CW00539053

Women's Writing

past and present

**Caroline
Zilboorg**

ST EDWARD'S SENIOR SCHOOL LIBRARY

Series Editor: Adrian Barlow

St. Edward's School Cheltenham

TE15447

CAMBRIDGE

ss

PUBLISHED BY THE PRESS SYNDICATE OF THE UNIVERSITY OF CAMBRIDGE
The Pitt Building, Trumpington Street, Cambridge, United Kingdom

CAMBRIDGE UNIVERSITY PRESS
The Edinburgh Building, Cambridge CB2 2RU, UK
40 West 20th Street, New York, NY 10011–4211, USA
477 Williamstown Road, Port Melbourne, VIC 3207, Australia
Ruiz de Alarcón 13, 28014 Madrid, Spain
Dock House, The Waterfront, Cape Town 8001, South Africa

http://www.cambridge.org

© Cambridge University Press 2004

This book is in copyright. Subject to statutory exception and to the provisions of relevant collective licensing agreements, no reproduction of any part may take place without the written permission of Cambridge University Press.

First published 2004

Printed in the United Kingdom at the University Press, Cambridge

Typefaces: Clearface and Mixage   *System:* QuarkXPress® 4.1

A catalogue record for this book is available from the British Library

ISBN 0 521 89126 4 paperback

Prepared for publication by Gill Stacey
Designed by Tattersall Hammarling & Silk
Cover illustration: Woman Writing (oil on canvas) by Pierre Bonnard (1887–1947), Bridgeman Art Library, London / Sonia Henie Collection, Norway

Contents

Introduction

Today women can be found writing about all sorts of subjects in all sorts of ways. The best-seller list in any newspaper contains female as well as male writers, as does any bookshop window. Even a quick click on www.amazon.co.uk offers you bright advertisements for writing by women that ranges from cookery books and 'how to' guides to treatises on government and new novels. Since women writers seem to be everywhere, how can we talk about a special category called 'women's writing'?

Indeed, many women writers – from the American poet Edna St. Vincent Millay (1892–1949) to the British novelist Iris Murdoch (1919–1999), the South African novelist Nadine Gordimer (b. 1923) and the Canadian author Margaret Atwood (b. 1939) – have gone so far as to reject the category of 'women writers'. Just reading a text probably will not reveal to you whether it was written by a woman or a man. So what difference does it make to think about an author's gender as you read? Does it make less or more of a difference for particular authors? Do you, for instance, read Emily Brontë (1818–1848) and Sylvia Plath (1932–1963) as woman writers, but not Jane Austen (1775–1817) or A.S. Byatt (b. 1936)? How does the period during which a woman writer wrote influence her work? Does it matter whom she was reading or whom she was writing for? In what ways do modern readers, aware of contemporary gender issues, read differently from earlier readers?

Focusing on texts written in English and emphasising writing by women from the beginning of the Renaissance period in the 1300s to the 21st century, *Women's Writing: Past and Present* tries to answer these questions. Since recent responses to women's writing have expanded the field of what we read and how we read it, this book illustrates not only the richness and diversity of female literary voices, but also the many changing and different contexts in which writing by women can be read.

How this book is organised

Part 1: Reading women writers
Part 1 presents a chronological examination of selected women writers, emphasising the historical and cultural experiences which directly and indirectly affected what they wrote about and the ways they expressed their thoughts and feelings.

Part 2: Approaching the texts
Part 2 examines the challenge of thinking and writing about women writers within a variety of contexts. It offers a number of examples for contextual reading as well as questions suitable for discussion and individual writing.

Part 3: Texts and extracts
Part 3 offers a diverse selection of women's writing covering several centuries. These passages from fiction and non-fiction, sections from longer poems and complete short poems illustrate the variety of women's literary expression. They also provide additional examples of writing rooted in the contexts described in Part 1.

Part 4: Critical approaches
This part explores the different ways that critics and readers have responded to women's writing.

Part 5: How to write about women writers
Part 5 considers the task of writing about literature by women. It offers guidelines and assignments for those for whom this book is chiefly intended: students reading women writers as part of an advanced course in literary studies.

Part 6: Resources
This part provides suggestions for further reading and advice on using information technology. It also includes a glossary of critical terms. (Terms which appear in the glossary are highlighted in bold type when they first appear in the main text.)

At different points throughout the book, and at the end of Parts 1, 2, 4 and 5, there are tasks and assignments which suggest a variety of contexts through which you might approach an understanding of particular works and issues.

1 | Reading women writers

- What is women's writing?

- Which female authors are important?

- What ideas, traditions and history are significant for understanding women's writing?

- How is literature by women separate or different from literature by men?

The difficulties facing women writers

There was a time when many readers might well have thought that there were almost no women writers. Until recently, in fact, literature by women was nearly excluded from the literary **canon**, those important works with which people were traditionally expected to be familiar. There were, of course, a few notable exceptions such as Jane Austen and the Brontës, but the statistics are startling. In his essay 'The Sociology of Authorship: The Social Origins, Education, and Occupations of 1,100 British Writers, 1800–1935' (1962, in *Writers, Readers, and Occasions: Selected Essays on Victorian Literature and Life*, 1989), Richard Altick discovered that, on the basis of books published in Britain between 1800 and 1935, the proportion of female to male writers was fairly consistent at a disappointing 20 per cent, but when one looks at anthologies and book lists for university and college courses – in other words, samples of work theoretically chosen on the basis of literary interest and merit – the statistics are even worse. In 1971, Tillie Olsen (b. 1913) noted that 'Achievement' as 'gauged by what supposedly designates it' came to 'one woman writer for every 12 men (8 per cent women, 92 per cent men)' (from *Silences*, 1978). Feminist efforts over the past 30 years have made a significant difference in the number of women writers published and in the number of texts by women included on courses, but representation is still far from equal for a great many reasons. Even in the *New Dictionary of National Biography* (2004), in which the proportion of women represented has doubled, the increase is only from five to ten per cent.

▶ Make your own survey about women writers included in (a) a bookshop display window; (b) a list of required or recommended books for a course; (c) a literary anthology; (d) a list of your own or a friend's favourite authors or books or stories or poems. What do these sources tell you about the attitudes, interests and values of their creators? What 'messages' about women's writing do they convey?

In her important book *A Room of One's Own* (1929), Virginia Woolf (1882–1941) pointed out that it is difficult to make a lasting name for oneself as a male or female writer in any age. A person needs to be literate for a start. In the centuries before the written word – and long afterwards, as well – there was, of course, an **oral tradition** of songs and poems, legends and stories, anecdotes and myths. These have come down to us as folklore or fairy tales, **ballads** and even **epics**, but they are preserved for us to read because someone somewhere at some point wrote them down. Those writers may or may not have remained nameless, but they are not the actual authors, the originators, of the texts they inscribed. Indeed, in 1897 Samuel Butler wrote an entire book arguing that the author of *The Odyssey* – which scholars now agree was probably an oral epic long before being written down in the 4th century BCE – was not in fact Homer, the blind male poet, but a female author (*The Authoress of the Odyssey: where and when she wrote, who she was, the use she made of the Iliad, & how the poem grew under her hands*). Virginia Woolf even contended, 'Anon, who wrote so many poems without signing them, was often a woman.'

In order for a text to endure, not only must its author or someone else write it down, but it must be published, and publication is seldom easy. Before the invention of the printing press in about 1440, 'publication' meant the careful copying out of a text by a scribe, who was usually paid by a nobleman for this work and who, by the early medieval period in Europe, may well have been a monk. This means of preserving a literary work meant that the nobleman or the Christian Church had to decide if the text were worth the time, care and money involved in this kind of publication. That is, a sort of filtering or censorship dependent on class, religious belief and gender became an inseparable part of the preservation of literary works.

▶ Look at an ancient or medieval manuscript. Many are available to view in museums or are reproduced in modern books, but you might also look at a selection reproduced on the Internet, for instance on such websites as:

- Early Manuscripts at Oxford University at
  http://image.ox.ac.uk

- Some Medieval Manuscripts at
  http://www.physics.ohio-state.edu/~prewett/medieval.html

- Royal Library of Copenhagen–Medieval Manuscripts at
  http://www.kb.dk/elib/mss/mdr/index-en.htm

What time and care do you think went into these manuscripts? What evidence do you find of the interests, status and values of the scribe who copied the text or the patron who paid for it? What is the particular text about? Who do you suppose read this text? What sort of author do you suppose wrote it? What can you conclude about it which might help you to understand women writers?

This 'censorship' did not end with the printing press and the more efficient means of printing that developed during the **Industrial Revolution** that followed. To get into print, many female authors took **pseudonyms**, that hid their identities. George Eliot (1819–1880), the name by which Mary Ann Evans is still known, took a male pseudonym. The Brontës' work originally appeared under pseudonyms that were intentionally ambiguous in gender: Charlotte (1816–1855), Emily (1818–1848) and Anne Brontë (1820–1849) initially published as Currer, Ellis and Acton Bell.

Even if a writer does manage to get published, however, there are the additional problems of reaching sympathetic readers and keeping a work in print. The first edition of poems by the Brontë sisters sold only two copies, while the Romantic poet John Keats (1795–1821) received so much negative criticism of his work that he was sure it would go out of print and no one would remember it. On his grave in Rome, the **epitaph** he requested appears under his name: 'Here lies one whose name was writ in water.' Many texts by women, because of adverse criticism or neglect, have gone out of print and are thus now 'lost' to us.

Sometimes women cannot finish their work or withhold it from publication. As the literary critic Ellen Moers points out at the very beginning of *Literary Women: The Great Writers* (1977), 'A woman's life is hard': she must often take care of the household, bear children, and serve her husband's needs – not activities that give a person the leisure and calm required for creative work. Under these circumstances, if a woman does write, she is apt to chose **genres** that many readers may not be used to considering as serious literature – for example, letters, diaries or travel journals. Indeed, as Woolf points out in *A Room of One's Own*, until recently many women who managed to write were childless – for instance, Jane Austen and the Brontës. Further, few female writers married, or if they did, they married late – for example, Charlotte Brontë and George Eliot. However, even when women did write, they were frequently prevented from finishing what they started: Tillie Olsen began her novel *Yonnondio* (1974) in the 1930s, but the demands placed upon her by the need to earn money, as well as to care for a family that eventually included six children, made her reluctantly put the work aside. When she finally published it 40 years later, she was unable to pick up where she had left off and the text remains unfinished. Emily Dickinson (1830–1886) left behind 1,775 completed poems, but only seven of these were published during her lifetime. None of these appeared in the form in which she had written them – editors changed her punctuation and even her individual words – so it is perhaps understandable that Dickinson carefully kept back the remaining 1,768 poems, stitched together in little booklets and stored secretly in a trunk in her bedroom.

Women writers may also feel that their work is not important, not worth publishing, preserving or even finishing at all. Consider, for instance, the implications for women's writing of such traditional advice to women as that offered by Ban Zhao (c. 45–110), a female teacher during the Han dynasty in China (see Part 3: Texts and extracts, page 80). The modern American poet Adrienne Rich has written of 'self-trivialisation' as one of the ways in which women writers throughout history have been taught to 'destroy themselves'. Specifically, Rich contends that women often fall into the trap of:

> … Believing the lie that women are not capable of major creations. Not taking ourselves or our work seriously enough; always finding the needs of others more demanding than our own. Being content to produce intellectual or artistic work in which we imitate men, in which we lie to ourselves and each other, in which we do not press to our fullest possibilities, to which we fail to give the attention and hard work we would give to a child or a lover.
>
> (from 'Anne Sexton: 1928–1974' [1974] in
> *On Lies, Secrets, and Silence: Selected Prose, 1966–1978*, 1979)

Throughout the ages, women have often been treated and taught to think of themselves as children; for example, in 1912, when the Titanic was sinking, the policy was 'women and children first'. Indeed, people have often thought that women, like children,' should be seen and not heard'.

In *How to Suppress Women's Writing* (1983), Joanna Russ (b. 1937) has written explicitly about the ways literature by women has been discounted. People have said such things as:

> *She didn't write it.*
> *She wrote it, but she shouldn't have.*
> *She wrote it, but look what she wrote about.*
> *She wrote it, but 'she' isn't really an artist and 'it' isn't really serious, of the right genre – i.e., really art.*
> *She wrote it, but she wrote only one of it.*
> *She wrote it, but it's only interesting/included in the canon for one, limited reason.*
> *She wrote it, but there are very few of her …*
> *She wrote it, but she doesn't fit in …*
> *She's wonderful, but where on earth did she come from?*

The contexts for women's writing

For many reasons texts by women cannot be considered outside the dominant literary tradition that includes texts by men. Certainly, throughout history, women writers have been aware of established literary conventions as well as of works by their male contemporaries. A woman writer looking for a role model finds numerous literary examples, among them the many female characters who are writers or speakers in texts by men: for instance, the Wife of Bath in Chaucer's *Canterbury Tales* (c. 1400); Shakespeare's Lady Macbeth; Samuel Richardson's Clarissa in his novel *Clarissa* (1748–1749); or James Joyce's Molly Bloom in *Ulysses* (1922). In fact, in literature written by men, female characters of all sorts – the Virgin Mary and Mary Magdalene in the Bible; Eve as she appears not only in the Bible but in John Milton's *Paradise Lost* (1667); Hester Prynne in Nathaniel Hawthorne's *The Scarlet Letter* (1850); Anna in Tolstoy's *Anna Karenina* (1873–1877); Emma in Gustave Flaubert's *Madame Bovary* (1857) – offer another context within which to consider writing by women, as do works by men written from a woman's point of view, for instance, Theodore Dreiser's *Sister Carrie* (1900) or Sinclair Lewis's *Main Street* (1920).

However, there is also the context of an often but not necessarily or completely alternative 'tradition' of women's writing. It is this tradition that Woolf insists on when she writes, in *A Room of One's Own*, '… we think back through our mothers if we are women' and asserts that 'if you consider any great figure of the past, like Sappho, like the Lady Murasaki, like Emily Brontë, you will find that she is an inheritor as well as an originator, and has come into existence because women have come to have the habit of writing …'. In other words, women's writing is both a part of the literature of any period *and* a counterpoint to it, even a separate body of writing. Cultural history and specifically literary history are thus inevitable contexts for understanding texts by female authors.

Early women writers

Classical Greek and Latin literature offers a context for later women writers just as these early literatures offer important background for an understanding of, for example, the Irish author James Joyce, who based his novel *Ulysses* on Homer's *Odyssey*. Women who wrote before the Renaissance drew on earlier traditions with which modern readers may be unfamiliar. Part of the fascination of these early authors lies in discovering the historical contexts we need in order to understand their values and views of the world, as well as their use of language and the genres in which they wrote.

Sappho

The ancient Greek poet Sappho (c. 620–550 BCE), who lived on the island of Lesbos, is often cited as the first and even the greatest woman writer. We know that she led a circle of female disciples, but we have little information about her. Her work survives only as two short poems and several fragments quoted by later admiring critics. We do know, however, that most of her writing was love poetry and that she wrote **epigrams**.

Consider the following translation, entitled 'To Atthis' (1914), by the English poet Richard Aldington (1892–1962). The poem is so close to a literal translation of the original that Aldington excluded it from his *Collected Poems* (1948):

> Atthis, far from me and Mnasidika,
> Dwells in Sardis;
> Many times she was near us
> So that we lived life well
> Like the far-famed goddess
> Whom above all things music delighted.
>
> And now she is first among the Lydian women
> As the mighty sun, the rose-fingered moon,
> Beside the great stars ...

This poem's intense and controlled emotion, expressed in language that seems wholly natural, is characteristic of Sappho's work, as is the subject: love, specifically here love between female friends. Yet which words in this poem suggest that knowledge of the ancient world might help us to understand it better? We might, for example, want to look at a map: Where is Sardis? Where is Lydia? Where is Lesbos? Thinking about where Sappho wrote, we might understand that when the word 'lesbian' is applied to Sappho, it carries more than one meaning, suggesting the island where she lived as well as her various feelings, as indicated in this poem, for the women who were her close friends. Reading Aldington's translation, we might also want to know more about the early Greeks' regard for music: Sappho's speaker clearly admires the goddess who delights in music (probably Athena), while the poet herself seems to value music as one of the highest arts. We might ask as well about Classical attitudes towards astronomy and astrology, for by comparing Atthis to 'the mighty sun' and 'the rose-fingered moon' and by placing her 'Beside the great stars', Sappho appears to be praising her very highly. We might also want to know more about the Greeks' attitudes towards love, and we might want to do some research on the subject of love poetry and specifically women's love poetry: what sort of literary tradition is there, for which Sappho may be the beginning? We may realise, too, that we cannot fully appreciate a poem if we have to rely on a translation.

Now consider the first two stanzas of 'Fragment Thirty- Six' (1924), by the American poet H.D. (Hilda Doolittle, 1886–1961), who married Richard Aldington in 1913. H.D.'s poem is a very free 'translation' and an expansion of a single line (*'I know not what to do: my mind is divided'*), all that we have of one of Sappho's verses:

I know not what to do,
my mind is reft:
is song's gift best?
is love's gift loveliest?
I know not what to do,
now sleep has pressed
weight on your eyelids.

Shall I break your rest,
devouring, eager?
is love's gift best?
nay, song's the loveliest:
yet were you lost,
what rapture
could I take from song?
what song were left?
(from *Collected Poems*, ed. Louis Martz, 1983)

Like 'To Atthis', 'Fragment Thirty-Six' seems to be about both love and music, but
unlike Aldington, who anchors his translation in a specific Classical time and place,
H.D. chooses to focus her version of Sappho on an inner conflict. While Aldington's
poem stresses the speaker's relationship with a female friend, in H.D.'s poem the
gender of the speaker and particularly of the sleeping lover are unclear. Since,
however, it seems that Sappho is the speaker of her fragment, we can infer that
H.D.'s speaker is also female, that she is – like Sappho and like H.D. – a woman
writer. But what is H.D.'s speaker divided about? Why should love and 'song' be in
conflict? In what ways may H.D. be speaking here about any woman writer's
conflict rather than only about Sappho's divided mind – or even her own? We may
not be able to answer these questions in a conclusive way, but the fact that H.D.'s
poem make us ask them emphasises Sappho's continuing significance and points
to a tradition of women writers confronting similar questions.

Translation

By focusing her energies on a text by Sappho in 'Fragment Thirty-Six', H.D.
associates her writing with Sappho's and places her own contemporary work
within a tradition of women's writing dating back to Sappho's time. Translation –
or even just reading earlier women writers seriously – helps to define a tradition of
women writers. In discussing the subject of translation in *Literary Women*, Ellen
Moers goes so far as to say that

> ... whoever wants to take the subject of women's love poetry
> seriously must know many languages, for the subject must carry
> them from Sappho to the saints, in the days when the poetry of
> spiritual love reveled in the imagery of marriage with Christ. There
> are French, Italian and Spanish women poets to be read seriously; and
> Russian would be absolutely essential, for Anna Akhmatova
> [1888–1966] used love poetry as her principal vehicle for ideas of a
> philosophical and historical cast.

Such efforts also make us aware of the long and rich historical context within which we can read later female authors and within which we can orient ourselves as female or male readers. For example, in order to write her poem 'Paula Becker to Clara Westhoff' (1975–1976) the American poet Adrienne Rich (b. 1929) translated letters between the German artist Paula Becker (1876–1907), married to the painter Otto Modersohn, and Clara Westhoff (1878–1954), her friend and fellow artist, who married the poet Rainer Maria Rilke (1875–1926). Rich's poem, a **dramatic monologue** told from Becker's point of view, reveals the artist's feelings as she anticipates the birth of her child: 'I didn't want this child./ You're the only one I've told./ I want a child, maybe, someday, but not now.' Becker realises that having a child will make painting more difficult for her, perhaps impossible. She is upset when she dreams that after her death Rilke will write a poem about her claiming her as his friend; in Rich's poem Paula tells Clara, 'I was your friend', and insists that Clara 'of all people/... will hear all I say and cannot say'. Rich makes her 'translation' even more powerful by placing it in its specific biographical context: she prefaces this poem with a short account of her 'characters', telling us that Paula Becker died in a haemorrhage after childbirth.

Male writers like Richard Aldington, who learnt at school the Greek he needed for 'To Atthis', also use translation as a way of situating their work within a larger historical context and within the established literary tradition. For example, Alfred Lord Tennyson (1809–1892), the popular Victorian poet laureate, based his 'Ulysses' (1842) on Homer's *Odyssey* and on Dante's account in *The Divine Comedy* (1305–1321), and presented his own narrative of the ancient hero's return to Greece. Later Tennyson retold the legend of King Arthur and his knights in his *Idylls of the King* (1869). More recently, the British poet laureate Ted Hughes (1930–1999) published translations of classical myths in his *Tales from Ovid* (1997) as well as a translation of a play by the 17th-century French dramatist Jean Racine, *Phaedra* (1998), while in 2000 the Irish poet Seamus Heaney (b. 1939), a Nobel Prize winner, published *Beowulf*, his poetic retelling of the Old English epic. Such efforts, however, by well-educated and highly regarded male writers at the peak of their careers seem qualitatively different from what women writers are doing.

Murasaki and Li Ch'ing-chao

It is not only the heritage of writing in English nor even the western literary tradition that provides a context for reading past and present women writers. Other cultures, as Moers indicates, have strong and influential traditions of literature, as the writing of The Lady Murasaki (978–1031), one of Japan's most admired authors, illustrates. Her long fictional work, *The Tale of the Genji*, tells of complex romantic relationships at the 11th-century Japanese court. Known widely in the west through translations, Murasaki's account reveals a skilful female author writing about the intricacies of courtship rituals as she analyses women's and men's roles in a highly conventional male-dominated society.

Li Ch'ing-chao (1084–1151), whose name in the western alphabet is sometimes spelled 'Li Qingzhao', is one of the most celebrated Chinese woman poets. Two centuries before the invention of the printing press in Europe, the Chinese had developed printing into an efficient art. Indeed, many social and economic changes in China at this time had an important impact on women's lives. As Patricia Buckley Ebrey points out in *The Cambridge Illustrated History of China* (1996): 'With printing and the expansion of the educated class, more women were taught to read and write. It was not at all uncommon in the educated class for wives to be able to write letters and tutor their young children.' Li Ch'ing-chao's poetry achieved a significant popularity; a modern critic, Liu Wu-chi, contends that her poems 'compare well with the works of her contemporaries, among whom, though a woman, she ranks supreme'. Indeed, she 'succeeded in depicting the emotions and vicissitudes of a young woman. Many Chinese poets have attempted to delve into the inner recesses of the female mind ... but they fall short in the presentation of a genuine woman's feeling with all its intimacy, delicacy and immediacy. In this respect, Li Ch'ing-chao's poems are unmatched.' (from *An Introduction to Chinese Literature*, 1966)

▶ Consider the two translations (Part 3, pages 80–81) of a poem by Li Ch'ing-chao, based apparently on her own experience as a young wife after her husband's departure from home. What differences do you notice in the two versions? Which one do you feel does a better job of capturing 'a genuine woman's feeling with all its intimacy, delicacy and immediacy'? What in Li Ch'ing-chao's poem seems part of her particular time and place? What seems to you especially characteristic of women's experience? What seems universal?

Julian of Norwich

As Moers suggests, readers examining the historical context of women's writing on love would need to look at women writers who focus not just on romantic love, as Murasaki and Li Ch'ing-chao do, but on the love of God and, in the West, specifically on writing about their own perceptions of their relationship to Jesus.

Saint Theresa of Ávila (1515–1582) is only one of many medieval and **Renaissance** women who portrayed themselves as 'brides' of Christ and who used the passionate language of love to explain their feelings towards God. Julian of Norwich (c. 1342–?) is one of the first female writers to write in English, and she described in *A Book of Showings* her direct experiences of God's goodness, which she received through a series of religious visions. Dame (or Mother) Julian uses the language of paternal and especially maternal love to express her feelings. Thus she writes:

> As truly as God is our Father, so truly is God our Mother …
> I understand three ways of contemplating motherhood in God. The first is the foundation of our nature's creation; the second is his taking of our nature, where the motherhood of grace begins; the third is the motherhood at work. And in that, by the same grace, everything is penetrated, in length and in breadth, in height and in depth without end; and it is all one love.
> (modernised by Edmund Colledge and James Walsh, from *A Book of Showings*, 1978)

Dame Julian's feminine **images** here may strike us as startling, but they are not so radical at they may at first seem. While 'mother Jesus' was in fact a fairly common idea in the medieval period, *A Book of Showings* is significant in emphasising the unique meaning that Jesus has for women, whose spirituality and creativity this author explains through images of conception, birth and nurturing.

Margery Kemp

Margery Kemp (1373?–1438?) was another early English female writer who wrote an account of her spiritual life, *The Book of Margery Kemp*, in which she chronicled her intimate relationship to God in personal and erotic terms. After 20 years of marriage and the birth of 14 children, Kemp left her husband and 'married' Christ, recounting her decision as well as her struggle to persuade her husband to renounce their union. The first English autobiography written in the **vernacular**, Kemp's account of her visions and pilgrimages as far as Jerusalem reveals its speaker as a feisty woman, clever and committed, forceful and intense. Her work gives readers a vivid sense not only of her own character but of daily life in 15th-century England. Consider this conversation between Kemp and her husband, as she tries to persuade him to allow her to dedicate herself to God:

> She then asked her husband what was the cause that he had not meddled with her for eight weeks, since she lay with him every night in his bed. He said he was made so afraid when he would have touched her, that he dare do no more.

> 'Now, good sir, amend your ways, and ask God's mercy ... I pray you grant me what I ask ... suffer me to make a vow of chastity at what bishop's hand God wills.'
>
> 'Nay', he said, 'that I will not grant you, for now may I use you without deadly sin, and then might I not do so.'

Finally Kemp offers her husband a crafty bargain:

> 'Sir, if it please you, ye shall grant me my desire, and ye shall have your desire. Grant me that ye will not come into my bed, and I grant you to requite your debts ere I go to Jerusalem. Make my body free to God so that ye never make challenge to me, by asking any debt of matrimony ...,

At last her husband agrees, saying, 'As free may your body be to God, as it hath been to me.' (from *The Book of Margery Kemp*, modernised by W. Butler-Bowden, 1936)

Kemp replaced her physical marriage to her husband with a mystical marriage to Jesus, and wore for the rest of her life a ring engraved 'Jesus Christ is my love'. Her spirited personality, forthright argument and clever use of language may well remind us of Chaucer's Wife of Bath. While women writers certainly have a tradition of their own, their work thus offers a context for reading work by men as well as by women.

Gender and genre

We are lucky to have the compelling autobiographies of Julian of Norwich and Margery Kemp, for neither woman actually wrote her work in her own hand; both dictated their accounts to scribes. The status of these women writers allowed them this privilege, for both were highly regarded for their dedication to God and found themselves in communities able to record their words. A few women, such as Queen Elizabeth I (1533–1603), were highly educated because of their class. Indeed, Elizabeth wrote verse as well as speeches, and much of her work has survived, including her letters, royal decrees and other official documents. Her speech to the troops assembled at Tilbury to repel the anticipated Spanish invasion in 1588, takes the form of an affectionate letter and begins 'My loving people'. She reveals that she has been advised not to lead her troops into battle 'for fear of treachery', but insists that despite her gender, she intends 'to live or die amongst you all'. While she begins by using the royal 'we' ('We have been persuaded ...'), she quickly shifts to the more powerful and personal 'I', and asserts:

> I know I have the body but of a weak and feeble woman; but I have the heart and stomach of a king, and of a king of England too, and think foul scorn that Parma [Italy] or Spain, or any prince of Europe, should

dare to invade the borders of my realm; to which rather than any dishonour shall grow by me, I myself will take up arms, I myself will be your general, judge, and rewarder of every one of your virtues in the field.

(from The Public Speaking of Queen Elizabeth,
ed. George P. Rice, Jr, 1951)

What sort of woman does Elizabeth seem to be here? How does she choose to portray herself? Do you think she really feels that she is 'weak and feeble'? Why does she say so?

▶ You might compare Queen Elizabeth's words and character here with those of Henry V as portrayed by Shakespeare (1564–1616), Elizabeth's contemporary, in his play, *The Life of King Henry V* (1599), Act IV, Scene III, lines 20–67. How do both Elizabeth and Shakespeare represent the relationship between a monarch and his or her people? What differences do you notice? In what ways is Elizabeth's speech to the troops at Tilbury a woman's speech? In what ways is Henry's address to his troops at Agincourt a man's speech?

Many ordinary women, eager to set down their thoughts and feelings not so much for posterity but in order to communicate with relatives or friends, chose genres other than autobiography or public addresses, and did not seek publication for their work. Dame Julian and Margery Kemp wanted other people to read their work and to learn from it; they had clear **didactic** purposes and wanted their writing to reach a wide audience. But many female writers, in the medieval and Renaissance periods just as today, wrote personal letters, recorded their experiences in diaries or journals written for themselves or for family members, or even inscribed their views on life or morality while writing out recipes for children or friends. Most of these literary works have not been preserved, or if by chance they have, they remain unpublished; many such texts are carefully protected as rare historical documents in special libraries and archives.

Before the rise of the middle class during the Industrial Revolution, before there was a wide reading public and before the invention of the novel as we know it in the 1700s, at a time in England when even most poetry was written and published by men, women writers often chose to express themselves in these other genres. Today, when we are used to reading fiction, drama, and poetry, we may find this sort of writing fragmentary or awkward, and it may feel odd to try to talk about Elizabeth's speech to her troops at Tilbury or other literary works that do not have, for instance, a clear plot or conventional characters. If, however, we pay close attention to the speakers in these texts and focus on the writers' use of language, we can begin to see how effective these authors were in capturing their experiences and conveying their emotional responses.

▶ Look at the diary entry by the American writer Lydia Maria Child (1802–1880) in Part 3, pages 91–92. A highly regarded editor and the author of 21 books, including a two-volume history of women, Child earned her living by writing. Married but without children, she lived simply in rural Massachusetts and worked for the rights of women and black people. What does her list reveal about her? How is her list organised? While it is hard to imagine arguing for this list's artistic merit, do you find it sad or admirable or eloquent? Many details in Child's diary entry reveal its particular context (19th-century America); what do you also find in it that seems to you universal?

The oral tradition

Literature began long before writing. What we would now call poetry probably first existed as songs. We can imagine, for instance, lullabies created and sung by generations of cave parents to generations of babies; we can imagine verse sung round ancient camp fires by hunters or soldiers. Some of these songs were later written down; indeed, it has been argued that *The Odyssey* was perhaps originally an epic sung by travelling **bards** who memorised it and passed it down, with variations, from generation to generation. Even today we are familiar with folk songs, many of which date back to medieval times, such as 'Greensleeves' or 'Barbara Allen'. The authors of these often moving works remain for the most part nameless, but if Virginia Woolf was right, many of these anonymous authors may well have been women. Certainly the subject matter and themes of many ballads, for example, place them firmly in the tradition of women's writing. Consider, for instance, the first stanza of a typical ballad, 'The Wife of Usher's Well':

> There lived a wife at Usher's Well
> > And a wealthy wife was she;
> She had three stout and stalwart sons,
> > And sent them o'er the sea.

What do you imagine will happen to these young men? Whose experience will this ballad explore? What will you feel for the wife at Usher's Well? The loss that you might anticipate will occur in this text has its greatest impact upon the female character mentioned in the title, who – like the poem's author – remains nameless, defined here only by her relationships with the men in her life. Like many of the poems by Sappho and Li Ch'ing-chao, this ballad is about love and loss, about female solitude and emotional response.

We find similar anonymous songs, many of them still sung in their original languages, among indigenous peoples throughout the world. The North American Chippewa, for instance, have a song entitled 'My Love Has Departed', which was transcribed and translated by the female musicologist Frances Densmore (1867–1957) in 1910:

A loon
I thought it was
But it was
My love's
Splashing oar

To Sault Ste. Marie
He has departed
My love
Has gone on before me
Never again
Can I see him

Ballads and other poems in the oral tradition document women's experience and may give us valuable insights into women's feelings and the ways they put those feelings into actions and words. We learn about a young woman who followed her lover into war in 'Pretty Polly Oliver' (Part 3, pages 85–86), while in 'Bonnie Annie' we learn about the guilt felt by an unmarried pregnant woman. 'Fair Janet' recounts the pain of a forced marriage in which the title character is killed after the birth of her illegitimate child; in the well-known 'Barbara Allen' a woman regrets her rejection of a man who loves her.

Rewriting the oral tradition

Folk tales and fairy stories also often have roots in the oral tradition. While the 17th-century French author Charles Perrault wrote the version of 'Cinderella' with which most of us are familiar, it is not original to him, and most of us are probably also aware of other versions, for example the Italian opera 'La Cenerentola' (1817) by Gioacchino Rossini or the 20th-century film version by Walt Disney. Such fairy and folk tales are indeed constantly told and retold, and some women writers feel they have an obligation to retell these narratives from a female or feminist perspective, suggesting that the story's significance may well lie in its possibly female authorship, its sometimes hidden female perspective, or its depiction of female experience.

For example, the British fiction writer Angela Carter (1940–1992) has retold a number of myths and fairy tales in her collections *The Bloody Chamber* (1979) and *American Ghosts and Old World Wonders* (1993), while the British poet Carol Ann Duffy (b. 1955) starts her collection *The World's Wife* (1999) with 'Little Red Cap', a poem based on the Grimm Brothers' early 19th-century version of the tale usually called in English 'Little Red Riding Hood'. Duffy's poem recasts this story as a rite of female initiation in which the speaker, 'Little Red Cap', seduces the wolf, learning from him not just about sex but about the elemental passions and psychological understanding that Duffy presents as essential to a writer. The speaker first meets the wolf 'At childhood's end'; he is reading a paperback in a pub, where he buys Little Red Cap her first drink. When the wolf breathes in her ear, the speaker learns her 'first lesson'– 'the love poem'. At the end of Duffy's version, Little Red Cap, who stays with the wolf for a decade before killing him, is empowered to be a writer: 'Out of the forest I come with my flowers, singing, all alone.'

Retelling such stories also allows a woman writer to place herself within a tradition of women writers or speakers. When Virginia Woolf came to write *A Room of One's Own*, she chose to write in the first person from the perspective of a woman who may seem on the one hand to be the author – the established feminist writer Virginia Woolf – and on the other hand a nameless narrator – a naive fictional alter-ego, a sort of 'dumb bunny' speaker whose confusion is a literary device that allows the author to reveal her ideas to us slowly and carefully.

This complex speaker does, however, actually have a name that is important to our understanding of her, even though this name is only revealed to us by implication throughout the text. For instance, we learn in the first chapter that the speaker's inquiry into the nature and history of women's experience, and particularly women's literary experience, is inspired because of the contrast she notices between men's and women's colleges at Oxbridge. At the women's college she visits, she is hosted by Mary Seton. We learn in the second chapter that Woolf's speaker has an aunt, Mary Beton, whose legacy of five hundred pounds a year allows the speaker the independence she needs in order to write. In the fifth chapter, the speaker examines contemporary writing by women, pulling a novel called *Life's Adventure* off her library shelf. This is, of course, a fictional novel which Woolf has made up to suit the purposes of her text; its author is likewise fictional, and Woolf calls her Mary Carmichael. We might well wonder at all these women called 'Mary'. Traditionally, as in the Bible, women have been presented with basically two ways of being: either like the Virgin Mary (pure, good, maternal, passive, and long-suffering) or like Mary Magdalene (sexual, not so good, ideally repentant but perhaps not, active, attractive yet ultimately rejected). But who are Woolf's Marys? We can in fact recognise them as characters in the 16th-century Scottish ballad whose title reveals Woolf's speaker's name: 'Mary Hamilton' (see Part 3, pages 81–83).

The ballad, much of it in the first person from Mary Hamilton's point of view, recounts the story of a seduction. A domestic servant, perhaps even one of Mary Queen of Scots' maids of honour, Mary Hamilton is 'courted' by 'the hichest Stewart of a' ', one of the queen's relatives. She becomes pregnant, then drowns her baby at birth. When her crime is discovered, Mary Hamilton is condemned to death by hanging.

► Most of the ballad is devoted to Mary Hamilton's reaction to her impending death. On the basis of the text, what were the circumstances of her seduction? Why do you think she killed the baby she calls 'bonny', 'wee' and 'sweet'? Why do you suppose she insists on 'robes o white'? What does the next to last stanza reveal about her relationship to the queen? Now look carefully at the final stanza. What is gained when the speaker brings in the other Marys here?

There is particular eloquence in the concluding two lines, which Woolf certainly had in mind while writing *A Room of One's Own*, for the ballad insists at its end on a community of 'Maries', a community of women. Woolf may expect us to think of other Marys, too – not only the Virgin Mary and Mary Magdalene, but even Queen Mary. The ballad ends, however, with an emphasis on the plight of Mary Hamilton herself, and its final word is 'me', drawing our attention to Mary Hamilton as the author of the poignant tale she is telling. By implying an association between her speaker and Mary Hamilton, Woolf suggests that Hamilton's situation is that of all women: potentially competent, assertive and independent, but in fact too often vulnerable, angry and victimised by the forces arrayed against them.

Woolf's **allusions** to 'Mary Hamilton' enrich *A Room of One's Own* by locating it within the larger context of women's writing, but female authors – like their male contemporaries – have not always been aware of this tradition. Indeed, many women writers in the years following the composition of 'Mary Hamilton' saw themselves as solitary pioneers, while their work, often compared unfavourably with that of men, had to struggle for publication.

Women writers of the 17th century

Mary Hamilton's anger and frustration with her limited control over her own life is not surprising. Despite exceptions, women in the 17th century did not enjoy most of the privileges granted to men. For instance, if there were no witness that a child had been born dead, mothers of stillborn babies could be, like Mary Hamilton, accused of infanticide – a law in effect in Britain until 1803. A woman in such a case was guilty until proven innocent. While unmarried women could own property and while a widow could inherit at least a portion of her husband's estate, a married woman was not even considered a person in her own right: she could not own property or make a will; she had no rights to her children, no right to divorce. A married woman did not even have rights over her own body: an Englishman was permitted to imprison his wife in their house until as late as 1891, and no married woman could accuse her husband of rape, for until the second half of the 20th century, a married man in Britain or America had the legal right to have sex with his wife whenever he wanted – indeed, she had no right to refuse.

Education, as Woolf points out in her story of Judith Shakespeare ('Judith

Shakespeare', Part 3, pages 94–95), was also a problem for women during this period, for unlike her male contemporaries, the 17th-century woman was denied access to the kind of education open to her brothers. Not only did fewer women than men learn to read and write at this time, all women were prevented from receiving the kind of education that men received. While British and American boys might learn Latin and Greek at school, giving them access to Classical history and literature, a girl's education, depending on her class, was more likely to occur at home and to consist of instruction in domestic arts such as sewing and cooking. While emphasis was placed on educating boys in mathematics and science, giving them access to knowledge about medicine and technology, girls were more likely to be taught music or embroidery. No young woman, whatever her class, had access to higher education: Oxford and Cambridge Universities were closed to women until the late 19th century, while Harvard University (founded in 1636) and Yale University (founded in 1701) did not admit women until late in the 20th century.

Such exclusion had a serious impact on the female writer. As the anonymous author of 'An Essay in Defence of the Female Sex' (1696) declared, because of their education, men had 'a vaster field for the imagination to rove in, and their capacities thereby enlarged'. At a time when women were usually seen as generally inferior to men – less rational, less intelligent, less knowledgeable, even less moral than men – women authors were widely criticised. Although writing was one of the few respectable ways for a middle-class woman to earn a living, the woman who wrote was often ridiculed for doing so. In *The Lady's New Year's Gift; or Advice to a Daughter* (1688) Lord Halifax declared that 'there is inequality in the sexes, and that for the better economy of the world, the men, who were to be the lawgivers, had the larger share of reason bestowed upon them.' The French satirist Jean de La Bruyère (1645–1696) went even further, concluding that women had no moral sense, while the French comic dramatist Jean Molière (1622–1673) satirised learned women in two of his plays, *L'École des Femmes* (1662) and *Les Femmes Savantes* (1672). Daniel Defoe (1660–1731), the English author of *Robinson Crusoe* (1719) and *Moll Flanders* (1722), was exceptional in arguing in his *Essay on Projects* (1697) for equal educational opportunity for women as well as men. Women writers of this period were well aware of the moral restrictions, cultural attitudes, and social conventions that worked against them.

Anne Bradstreet

Anne Bradstreet (1612–1672) wrote the first book of poems to be composed in the New World, *The Tenth Muse, Lately Sprung Up in America* (1650), which quickly became popular on both sides of the Atlantic. Supposedly published without her consent by her brother-in-law while he was on a trip to London, this collection of verse is astonishing in its emotional power, erudition, and frequently personal frame of reference. Bradstreet's writing reveals a number of important influences, among them her Puritan beliefs, the challenges she faced in a new land, and her own family.

Born in England to wealthy parents, Bradstreet was tutored at home and allowed to read widely. At the age of 16, she married Simon Bradstreet, a staunch Puritan educated at Cambridge University, and arrived in America two years later in 1630. There she encountered the dangers of starvation and disease, witnessed attacks by Native Americans, and gave birth to eight children. Although throughout her life she was a faithful Puritan and a dutiful wife and mother, Bradstreet frequently revealed her mixed feelings about the male authorities in her life, including God, the men in her family, and both the male authors who were her models and the male readers who had the potential to be her critics. While Bradstreet wanted their approval, she also rebelled, as her verse shows, against their view of women's experience and abilities as being limited and unimportant.

▶ Look at 'The Author to Her Book' (1678), a poem Bradstreet wrote as a preface to the second edition of *The Tenth Muse* (Part 3, page 83). How does Bradstreet feel about seeing her verse in print? Why do you suppose Bradstreet calls her book 'Thou ill-formed offspring of my feeble brain'? What sorts of images in this poem show you that the author thinks of her book as her child? Why do you think she declares that 'At thy return [from England in printed form] my blushing was not small'? Do you entirely believe her claims that she feels her book is flawed and awkward, that she herself is a 'poor' author? Why would she say so?

We probably cannot take literally Bradstreet's assertion in 'The Author to Her Book' that she is a reluctant and unskilled writer, calling upon her readers' tolerance of what she insists is literary awkwardness. In fact, it is a convention for authors to claim that their work has faults for which they alone are to be blamed or that their work is at most a modest contribution to the literary tradition. For example, at the end of his epic masterpiece *Troilus and Criseyde*, Geoffrey Chaucer (c. 1343–1400) wrote:

> Go, little book …
> … and on no man's work look enviously
> But be a servant of all poetry,
> And kiss the steps their passing has made gracious –
> Virgil, Ovid, Homer, Lucan, and Statius.
>   (Book V, lines 1786–1792, modernised by F.N. Robinson, ed.,
>   *The Riverside Chaucer*, 1987)

Thanking others is also part of this convention. For instance, in *Savage Beauty: The Life of Edna St. Vincent Millay* (2001), the accomplished biographer Nancy Milford states, 'I owe a great deal to many people.' She asks, 'where would I be without ... sustaining friendship?' She lists people who 'have pulled' her 'out of a mess with style', who have corrected her bad spelling and 'helped' her 'to believe' in her book. She also thanks her family for their support and mentions other women writers whose example have made her writing possible, specifically Lois Gould ('... my world would be a lesser place if she were not writing in it') and Toni Morrison (b. 1931), whose 'advice and support and, most crucially, her own model of a continuing literary life have meant the world to me'. Bradstreet's claims of unworthiness have particular significance, however, because by writing she is violating the conventions of her time and place.

▶ Consider Anne Bradstreet's 'The Author to Her Book' (Part 3, page 83) within this convention of humility and acknowledgement. What does her poem share with Chaucer's? What does her poem share with Milford's 'Acknowledgements'? How is Bradstreet's poem and situation different from those of this earlier male writer and this female writer who wrote over three centuries later?

Thinking back to a female predecessor, Anne Bradstreet wrote 'In Honour of That High and Mighty Princess Queen Elizabeth of Happy Memory' (1650). Queen Elizabeth I had died nearly 50 years earlier, but Bradstreet made sure that her first book of poems included a vivid portrayal of an accomplished woman, a female figure she called 'Our Amazon in th'Camp of Tilbury'. At the time of the poem's composition, Elizabeth Tudor lay dead and 'in silence', but Bradstreet claims, she was 'so good, so just, so learn'd, so wise' that 'From all the kings on earth she won the prize.' Bradstreet then defends her claim:

> Nor say I more than duly is her due,
> Millions will testify that this is true.
> She hath wiped off th'aspersion of her sex,
> That women wisdom lack to play the rex.
> (from Anne Bradstreet *The Complete Works*, ed. Joseph McElrath
> and Allen Robb, 1981)

What do you learn about Bradstreet from her portrait of Queen Elizabeth? What does her tribute to the queen gain from the poet's calling Elizabeth an 'Amazon'? Why does Bradstreet write that 'Millions will testify' to what she claims? What is gained here by her rhyming 'sex' and 'rex' (the Latin word for 'king')? At first it may seem difficult to reconcile the author of this poem with the author of 'The Author to Her Book', but to be a woman writer in the 17th century was indeed to be a contradiction, even a rebel.

Aphra Behn

Aphra Behn (1640–1689) led quite a different life from Anne Bradstreet, and is often remembered as the first woman to have made a living by her writing. Behn was not a 'respectable' woman in a number of ways. She scandalised her contemporaries by her irreverent works, many of which were openly sexual and even bawdy, and she was considered just as outrageous for achieving her own economic independence in spite of both her female sex and her middle-class background. Virginia Woolf states that Behn's achievement in making 'enough to live on', made her a model for subsequent women writers, 'for here begins the freedom of the mind, or rather the possibility that in the course of time the mind will be free to write what it likes'. Yet Behn was a threatening and upsetting role model, for while girls who wanted to write might now argue that they could earn money by doing so, their parents, as Woolf explains, would likely be quick to answer, 'Yes, by living the life of Aphra Behn! Death would be better!' (from *A Room of One's Own*).

Unlike her wealthy literary contemporaries – such as Lady Mary Chudleigh (1656–1710), Anne Killigrew (1660–1685), Margaret Cavendish, Duchess of Newcastle (1623–1673), and Anne Finch, Countess of Winchelsea (1661–1720) – Aphra Behn lived by her wits. We do not know who her parents were, but as a girl she travelled to the West Indies with a foster family. When she returned to England in 1664, she married a merchant, Mr Behn, who apparently died the following year. In 1666, Aphra Behn served as a spy in Antwerp, but by 1668 she was in a debtors' prison. In 1670 her first play, *The Forced Marriage*, was produced on the London stage. Behn went on to a remarkable literary career, writing and publishing 14 plays, a number of poems, and four novels, among them *Oroonoko* (1688), an anti-slavery narrative set in Surinam.

Sex and gender are at the heart of much of Behn's work. In the preface to her play *The Lucky Chance* (1687), she writes of 'my masculine part, the poet in me', while in an epilogue to another play, *Sir Patient Fancy* (1678), she asks explicitly, 'What has poor woman done, that she must be/ Debarred from sense and sacred poetry?' If a woman were a writer in the 17th century, she was regarded as not only unfeminine but masculine, even no longer a woman or a mad woman. The act of writing made her seem to her contemporaries unfit for her role as a woman in her society.

Despite this conflict, however, Behn persevered, and flaunted not only her literary skills but both her female gender and her sexuality. In 'The Willing Mistress' (1673), for example, a servant confesses that she and her lover have been willing partners:

> ... many kisses did he give
>> And I returned the same,
> Which made me willing to receive
>> That which I dare not name.

In her poem 'The Disappointment' (1680), Behn tells the story of the passionate Cloris and the 'amorous Lysander'. Quite explicit about their love-making, Behn includes a great many specific details, describing the two lovers 'Ready to taste a thousand joys'. Unfortunately, however, Lysander finds himself 'Unable to perform'. Cloris is keenly disappointed:

> Finding that god of her desires
> Disarmed of all his awful fires ...
> The blood forsook the hinder place,
> And strewed with blushes all her face,
> Which both disdain and shame expressed ...

Cloris flees 'Lysander's arms'. Behn sympathises with 'The nymph's resentments', and even feels a bit sorry for poor Lysander, yet the poem ends not with the frustrated lovers but with Lysander's anger:

> He cursed his birth, his fate, his stars;
> But more the shepherdess's charms,
> Whose soft bewitching influence
> Had damned him to the hell of impotence.

This poem is flirtatious and humorous throughout, but Behn concludes on a satiric note as the man blames the woman for his own 'disappointment'.

▶ What is Behn's point here? Why do you suppose she describes both her male and female characters as equally passionate? In what ways does this poem reveal Behn's protest against her society?

Woolf rightly called Behn 'shady and amorous', but she also admired Behn and insisted that 'All women together ought to let flowers fall upon the tomb of Aphra Behn ... for it was she who earned them the right to speak their minds.' (from *A Room of One's Own*)

Women writers of the 18th century

Samuel Johnson (1709–1784), one of the most admired writers of his day, wrote with a sense of the moral and intellectual responsibilities of authorship, yet he mocked the woman writer who attempted to earn her living by her pen, declaring that a woman writer was like a dancing dog: someone whose achievements were against her nature and even absurd, worthy of attention merely as a curiosity. The English poet Alexander Pope (1688–1744) went so far as to insist that women have no characters at all. In his play, *Three Hours After Marriage* (co-authored in 1713 with John Gay and John Arbuthnot), Pope directed his criticism specifically against woman writers, satirising Anne Finch as the mad poetess Phoebe Clinket. In his *Moral Essays*, 'Epistle II: To a Lady' (1735), Pope attacked the learned author Lady Mary Wortley Montagu (1689–1762) with cruel bitterness, accusing her of being a slovenly 'Sappho'.

Pope is clearly denigrating a line of women writers who might trace a tradition back to Sappho; indeed, by calling Lady Mary Wortley Montagu 'Sappho', Pope suggests that she is not to be taken seriously because of her feminist and even possibly 'lesbian' concerns. In such an atmosphere, to be a woman writer was almost a contradiction in terms, as Lady Mary Chudleigh pointed out in her poem 'To the Ladies' (1703). Insisting that 'Wife and servant are the same', she argued that through marriage men dominated women to the point where

> ... but to look, to laugh, or speak,
> Will the nuptual contract break.
> Like mutes she signs alone must make,
> And never any freedom take:
> But still be governed by a nod,
> And fear her husband as her God:
> Him still must serve, him still obey,
> And nothing act, and nothing say ...

Notice the number of words in this poem that suggest that a woman's only option is silence. Of course, there is **irony** here, too, for in 'To the Ladies' a female author is speaking out in a published text.

Contradictions such as this came to characterise much of what women wrote and much of what they wrote about; indeed, as late as the 1920s Virginia Woolf was capable of strategic dissembling – pretending to be ignorant and even simple at times in *A Room of One's Own* – in order to achieve her literary ends and give voice to her feminist concerns. Look, for instance, at the passage entitled 'The Manx Cat' (Part 3, page 93). Woolf portrays her narrator here, enjoying a delicious meal at a Cambridge college (probably Kings College, in about 1928), as a rather silly person: looking for an ashtray and failing to find one, noticing the cat but not saying exactly why it seems important to her, musing apparently at random, then laughing out loud and covering her embarrassment with what she presents as a chance observation. But what is Woolf actually saying? She implies some parallel between women humming and a tail-less cat: how are the two similar?

▶ What do you think Woolf is saying when she observes 'It is strange what a difference a tail makes'? How does her last statement in this passage serve to hide the seriousness of her feminist point? What use does Woolf make of irony and **satire** in the passage? Consider what is added to your understanding of this passage by knowing that a few pages earlier Woolf's narrator is chased off a college quadrangle by an official who explained in 'horror and indignation' that 'I was a woman. This was the turf; there was the path. Only the Fellows and Scholars are allowed here; the gravel is the place for me.' What does it add to your understanding that Woolf in *A Room of One's Own* cites both Johnson and Pope on the subject of female authors? How are Woolf's comments on the Manx cat enriched by your reading them in the context of what these 18th-century men had to say about women writers?

We can see similar contradictions in the life and work of Fanny Burney (1752–1840), who went on to write several novels, including her very successful *Evelina* (1778). At the age of 15, Burney burned all of her early writing because her stepmother convinced her that writing would make her less eligible for marriage in polite English society. Soon after, however, Burney began a secret diary, addressed to 'Miss Nobody' because only to 'Nobody' did she feel she could write.

The situation was somewhat different for women in 18th-century America. For example, in the colonies class was a less rigid and explicit category than in Europe, while America's struggle for political independence had roots in humanist notions of equality of rights and opportunities. Thus Abigail Adams (1744–1818) wrote to her husband, John Adams, as he was composing the 'Declaration of Independence' in 1776:

> ... I desire you would Remember the Ladies, and be more generous and favourable to them than your ancestors. Do not put such unlimited power into the hands of the Husbands. Remember all Men would be tyrants if they could. If perticuliar care and attention is not paid to the Ladies we are determined to foment a Rebelion, and will not hold ourselves bound by any Laws in which we have no voice, or Representation.

Cleverly, Abigail Adams uses in support of her feminist cause the same political language that male colonists were using to argue against British rule. While she also uses a degree of humour in an effort to persuade her husband, such words as 'unlimited power', 'tyrants', 'Rebelion, 'voice' and 'Representation' would have reminded him of the very serious parallels between the status and rights of women and those of Americans, both male and female, exploited by the colonial government.

Much as he loved his wife and much as their marriage was one in which Abigail Adams felt free to speak her mind, John Adams refused her request. He argued that if women were granted their rights, it would be too great a 'loosening' of the 'bands' of government; everyone in America would claim equal freedoms – including children, apprentices, 'Indians', and 'Negroes'. Granting rights to women would weaken the colonists' power to argue with Britain, he suggested, and the freedom she was requesting would bring about a far more radical equality than he and his fellow politicians – among them Benjamin Franklin as well as the slave-holding southerners Thomas Jefferson and George Washington – could afford to consider. Finally, his reaction was one of scorn and ridicule: he called his wife 'saucy' and declared, 'I cannot but laugh.' (from *The Book of Abigail and John: Selected Letters of the Adams Family, 1762–1784*, ed. L.H. Butterfield, 1975)

Women's education

In *A Room of One's Own*, Virginia Woolf argued that a woman needs, above all, two things in order to write: five hundred pounds a year (worth a great deal more in 1929 than now) and a room of her own. By 'five hundred pounds a year' Woolf meant sufficient funds so that a woman would not need to worry about earning her living – traditionally as a laundress, perhaps, or a domestic servant, a wet-nurse or even a prostitute; by the 1920s in Britain the jobs a woman might hold included work as a clerk, a nurse, a teacher or a factory worker – for until recently the possible wage-earning positions a woman might hold were quite limited, as indeed they continue to be even today in many parts of the world. An independent income would also free a woman from the necessity of marrying in order to achieve a measure of financial security. Woolf also stressed that, in addition to money, a woman would need 'a room of her own' a private and peaceful space in which to read, think, reflect and write. We might think of how we use the word 'space' today – as in 'I need some space '– suggesting just the necessary apartness and period of 'time out' that Woolf is writing about here. But of course neither money nor privacy would help a woman who did not know how to read or write.

The need for literacy increased rapidly in 18th-century Europe and America. During the 17th century, Puritans had been especially concerned that children of both sexes learn to read the Bible, but before the Industrial Revolution, most people lived in rural communities and had little need to read and write. During the 18th century, however, the population of cities increased and reading as well as writing became important tools in the workplace. By the middle of the century, a rational view of the universe – including the notion that God was like a great clockmaker, who had made a world based on perfect scientific principles – began to displace more traditional religious ideas. The English writer Mary Astell (1666–1731) used rational argument to show that women's apparent lack of ability resulted not from any inherent intellectual incapacity but from the lack of an adequate education. In *A Serious Proposal to the Ladies, for the Advancement of their True and Greatest Interest* (1694), she wrote, 'Instead of inquiring why all Women are not wise and good, we have reason to wonder that there are any so. Were the Men as much neglected, and as little care taken to cultivate and improve them, perhaps they wou'd be so far from surpassing those whom they now despise, that they themselves wou'd sink into the greatest stupidity and brutality.' Astell concluded that female mental 'incapacity, if there be any, is acquired, not natural' (from *Women in the Eighteenth Century*, ed. V. Jones, 1990).

Many philosophers during the 18th century, often now called 'The Age of Reason', would have agreed with Astell that women possessed the same intellectual potential as men, the same capacity for 'reason', and ought to be given similar educational opportunities. John Locke in Britain and Jean Jacques Rousseau in France were among the male thinkers who advocated women's education, and it is important to realise that such writers as Pope and Johnson reacted negatively towards women writers at least in part because they felt threatened by the changes occurring in their society. Virginia Woolf concluded in *A Room of One's Own* that when a man 'insisted a little too emphatically upon the inferiority of women, he was concerned not with their inferiority, but with his own superiority'. Illustrating Woolf's point, the modern American writer Erica Jong (b. 1942) has gone so far as to suggest that Pope's denigration of women writers also has its roots in his sense of physical inadequacy: because of a spinal infection in childhood, he grew to an adult height of only 4 feet 6 inches (137 centimetres) and became a hunchback.

▶ Look at Jong's satiric portrait of Pope in her novel *Fanny* (1980) in Part 3 (pages 103–104). What other reasons does she suggest for men's hostility towards women writers? What does this passage tell you about what women – and especially aspiring women writers – had to contend with during this period?

The expansion of the printed word

Readers and writers were able to use their skills during their leisure time as well as in the workplace, and this growing market encouraged a huge expansion of printed material. Statistics in America reflect important changes occurring at the same time in Britain and throughout Europe. For instance, between 1790 and 1830, nearly 400 'female academies' were founded, teaching reading and writing as well as domestic skills. By 1800, between 80 and 90 per cent of all women in New England could read, while by 1850, the rate of literacy among women in the United States approached that of men. New readers, many of them female, meant a larger audience for published material; a larger audience meant there was a need for more writers, many of them women. In America, the number of newspapers doubled during the Revolution (1776–1790), then tripled during the final decade of the 18th century. More female readers also meant that the kinds of material that got published changed significantly: newspapers printed poetry, stories, and articles addressed to women; new journals developed specifically aimed at a female audience; while book publishers printed what they felt women particularly would buy – novels, women's histories, conduct manuals and cookery guides. All of these printed materials also provided a new outlet for women writers.

Phyllis Wheatley

The black American poet Phyllis Wheatley (c. 1753–1784) was one of many women empowered by learning to read and write. She is a particularly interesting example because of her race and class, for reading and writing allowed her to move beyond the boundaries of her colour and her social position as a slave in domestic service. Born free in Senegal, the girl who was to be called Phyllis Wheatley was kidnapped by slavers and transported to Boston in Massachusetts at the age of five or six. In 1761, she was bought by John Wheatley, a successful merchant, whose family quickly discovered her intelligence and began to educate her. She learned to speak and to write English within her first 16 months in America, and went on, through informal lessons, to gain a good deal of knowledge, particularly of the Bible and the classics. In 1773, she was freed from slavery and travelled with the Wheatley family to London, where she was labelled 'The Sable Muse' and published her first volume of verse. After her return to America in 1774, she married a free black man, and bore three children, all of whom died in infancy. Her last years were spent in poverty, and she died at about the age of 30 in 1784.

Wheatley's African identity and education is reflected in her verse. In 'On Being Brought from Africa to America' (1773), she asserts that ''Twas mercy brought me from my pagan land' because 'Once I redemption neither sought nor knew.' Now, however, she has learned about 'God' and her 'Saviour'. She concludes that although some people scorn the 'sable race', 'Christians' ought to remember that 'Negroes black as Cain/ May be refined and join the angelic strain.' Similarly, in 'To the University of Cambridge, in New England' (1773), she begins:

> While an intrinsic ardor prompts to write,
> The muses promise to assist my pen;
> 'Twas not long since I left my native shore
> The land of errors, and Egyptian gloom …

Wheatley addresses university students in this poem and reminds them of the privilege of their education, but insists that knowledge of the Bible and rejection of 'sin' are even more important. She warns her audience by saying, 'An Ethiope tells you …'.

While Wheatley's poems may seem to us rather awkward and rough, even repetitive and formulaic, contemporary readers were impressed with her achievement – she did, after all, take Pope's poetry as her model. Wheatley always insisted on a Christian point of view and quite conventionally invoked the muses for inspiration, but she also emphasises throughout her verse her identity as an American woman of colour and her calling as a writer. Her early death reminds us of how precarious her situation was: as a free black woman, she had no economic security and was dependent on her husband, who turned out to be ambitious but irresponsible. In America at the end of the 18th century, Wheatley had neither the patronage nor the audience available to Aphra Behn; as a woman with young children, it would not have been possible for her to make her own living by her writing.

Early British feminism

The 18th century was a time of tremendous social change on both sides of the Atlantic, allowing many writers to develop feminist positions that would have earlier been impossible. Consider, for instance, Lady Mary Wortley Montagu's radical views of female education in the letter to her daughter (Part 3, pages 84–85).

▶ What sorts of learning does Lady Montagu think appropriate for her grand-daughter? What advantages does education offer a woman? What are the disadvantages? You might note that Montagu reveals her antagonism towards Pope. What evidence do you find in this passage that she herself has had a difficult time as a woman writer in her society? What are her 'two cautions'? Why does she offer these warnings?

Mary Wollstonecraft

The English feminist Mary Wollstonecraft (1759–1797) published her famous *A Vindication of the Rights of Woman* in 1792. This long essay presents the first extensive feminist criticism of the negative images of women in literature as well as the first fully developed argument for women's political, economic and legal equality. Wollstonecraft argues for women's rights and against the wrongs the author sees inflicted upon women in her society. She claims that women have been trivialised by a culture that advocates feminine inferiority. As a literary text on its own terms, *A Vindication* is eloquent. Over a hundred years before Virginia Woolf, Wollstonecraft asserts her 'profound conviction that the neglected education of my fellow-creatures is the grand source of the misery I deplore' and criticises the 'false education' women have received 'from the books written on this subject by men who, considering females rather as women than human creatures, have been more anxious to make them alluring mistresses than affectionate wives and rational mothers'.

▶ What words does Wollstonecraft use here for 'women' and their possible roles? What does the author gain by referring to women as 'fellow-creatures'?

Wollstonecraft goes on to criticise the sort of female behaviour and thinking that her culture advocates for women, claiming 'that elegance is inferior to virtue, that the first object of laudable ambition is to obtain a character as a human being, regardless of the distinction of sex'. She explains:

> Women are told from their infancy, and taught by the example of
> their mothers, that a little knowledge of human weakness, justly
> termed cunning, softness of temper, outward obedience, and a
> scrupulous attention to a puerile kind of propriety, will obtain for
> them the protection of man; and should they be beautiful, everything
> else is needless, for, at least, twenty years of their lives.

To understand what this early feminist is saying here, you might think of a top model or a popular female singer or actress: to what degree does Wollstonecraft's description of what women have been told for centuries account for the kind of public image of womanhood that these celebrities portray? You might also think about how women are portrayed in advertising on television and in magazines: what sorts of 'role models' are being offered to women?

Wollstonecraft is not only elegant in expressing her convictions in writing, she directs her attention to the importance of literature in women's lives. Like many of her contemporaries, both male and female, she was disturbed by the influence that sentimental and sensational fiction could have, especially on female readers. Just as many people are now disturbed by the depiction of sex and violence on television, fearing that viewers will be encouraged to become sexual or violent in ways unacceptable to their society, people in the 18th and 19th centuries were deeply suspicious of the negative effects they attributed to the novel. Wollstonecraft writes that 'Ignorant women, forced to be chaste to preserve their reputation, allow their imagination to revel in the unnatural and meretricious scenes sketched by the novel writers of the day.' She concludes this part of her essay with words that reveal not only her high literary standards, but her own deep feelings and rebellious personality:

> ... the reading of novels makes women, and particularly ladies of
> fashion, very fond of using strong expressions and superlatives in
> conversation; and, though the dissipated artificial life which they lead
> prevents their cherishing any strong legitimate passion, the language
> of passion in affected tones slips for ever from their glib tongues,
> and every trifle produces those phosphoric bursts which only mimic
> in the dark the flame of passion.

▶ What does the author mean here by 'mimic in the dark'? What reasons does she give in her essay for her assertion that novel-reading women cannot feel the real 'flame of passion'?

Mary Wollstonecraft's life reveals contradictions only hinted at in her work, and it is important to recognise the pressure society can have on individuals and the passions that individuals, perhaps especially gifted and radical thinkers, bring to their experiences. Unlike the frequently aristocratic female writers who were her contemporaries, Wollstonecraft came from a middle-class background. Her family, often in debt and moving from place to place, was unsupportive of her desire for education, and she had to acquire her learning on her own. She formed several very important friendships with other women, and earned her living through teaching and writing. Her ideas led her to France, where she went to witness the French Revolution and to escape from a failed love affair with the romantic painter Henry Fuseli. In Paris, she met and fell in love with the unscrupulous American writer Gilbert Imlay, but despite the birth of their daughter Fanny in 1794, she refused on principal to marry him, feeling that marriage was an institution that both exploited women and served the interests of the state. When Imlay abandoned Wollstonecraft during the Reign of Terror, she fled from Paris to London where, depressed at the discovery of her lover's infidelity, she attempted suicide by jumping off a bridge into the Thames. With determination, she recovered her spirits, and in 1796 took a new partner, this time a man equally committed to her ideas, the philosopher and novelist William Godwin. When she became pregnant, however, they decided to marry despite their shared convictions. A year later, Wollstonecraft died tragically, at the age of 36, from an infection that followed the birth of her second daughter, Mary Wollstonecraft Godwin. It was Wollstonecraft's life, as well as the often turbulent lives of other women writers, that inspired Virginia Woolf's agonised question in *A Room of One's Own*: '... who shall measure the heat and violence of the poet's heart when caught and tangled in a woman's body?'

▶ Woolf also recognised that the material conditions of life had a significant effect on women's experience. Look at the passage entitled 'The Spider's Web' (Part 3, page 94). How is fiction like a spider web? What do you suppose Woolf means when she writes that the spider's web of imaginative work can be 'pulled askew' or 'hooked up at the edge' or 'torn in the middle'?

▶ At the time of her death, Mary Wollstonecraft left behind an unfinished novel with a poignant title: *Maria; or, The Wrongs of Women*. Keeping in mind what you know about her life, how was her ability to work as an imaginative writer attached to what Woolf calls 'grossly material things'? How was Wollestonecraft's 'imaginative work' affected by her 'health and money' as well as by 'the houses' she lived in?

WOMEN'S WRITING: PAST AND PRESENT

Mary Shelley

Wollstonecraft's second daughter grew up to become the writer we know as Mary Shelley (1797–1851). She, too, was affected by 'the conditions' Woolf suggests in her passage about the spider's web. Mary grew up with her half sister in her father's household. William Godwin remarried when Mary was four, and his second wife had two children from a previous marriage. Mary grew up feeling like an outsider, longing for her absent mother and educating herself through reading in her parents' large library.

In 1814, at the age of 17, Mary met the dashing Romantic poet Percy Bysshe Shelley in London. Although he was already married to Harriet Westbrook, within a month, they confessed their feelings for one another at Mary Wollstonecraft's grave, where Mary regularly went to pay homage to her mother's memory. When Mary became pregnant, she and Shelley fled together to the Continent. Their first child, a little girl born prematurely, died at the age of two weeks. In 1816, Mary's half sister Fanny Imlay and Shelley's wife, Harriet Shelley, both committed suicide. Although they had little money, Mary Godwin and Percy Bysshe Shelley then married. For the rest of their life together, they travelled extensively, meeting other Romantic writers and enjoying a wide circle of friends. Mary Shelley gave birth to two more children, William, in 1816, and Clara in 1817. In 1818 she published her famous gothic novel *Frankenstein*. Later that year, Clara died of dysentery in Venice; in Rome in 1819, at the age of three, William also died. Mary's Shelley's last child, Percy, was born later the same year. In 1822, Percy Bysshe Shelley drowned.

Mary Shelley outlived her much-loved husband, with whom she had shared both a commitment to human rights and a passion for literature. She also outlived many of their close friends, among them John Keats, who died in 1821, the Romantic poet George Gordon, Lord Byron (1788–1824), and her own father, who died in 1836. She did not stop writing, however, and her work includes stories, five more novels, essays, travel sketches, journals, and biographies, as well as an extensively annotated edition of her husband's verse. Much of her writing, like *Frankenstein*, reveals the 'spider's web' to which it was inevitably attached: Mary Shelley wrote about isolated figures, about creativity and motherhood, about poverty and the struggle to gain an education, and about the difficulties of making one's way in the world when confronting prejudice and inevitable physical realities.

Women writers of the 19th century

The English novelist Jane Austen (1775–1817) began her novel *Pride and Prejudice* (1813) with a sentence that is now famous: 'It is a truth universally acknowledged that a single man in possession of a good fortune must be in want of a wife.' (The opening paragraphs of this novel appear in Part 3, pages 86–87). You may find this a humorous statement on several counts. By whom is Austen's assertion probably 'acknowledged', men or women? And why would anyone assume that a man with money needs a wife? Who will in fact benefit most from a wealthy man's marriage?

Since women in the 19th century continued to be denied the education their brothers received, their hopes for an adult future lay in making a 'good' marriage. Without such financial security, a woman would continue to be a 'child', reliant on her father's income and good will, confined to her parents' home and dependent on her parents' will. Without an economically sensible marriage, a woman could neither bring up her children responsibly nor have a measure of independence for herself. It is no surprise, then, that 'the marriage plot' was central to most 19th-century novels, and especially to those by women writers.

Austen's famous opening sentence is humorous but also sharply observant, even satirical. She is, of course, making fun of people – most likely women – who assume that rich men are looking for a wife to share the benefits of their fortunes, but she is also satirising early 19th-century English society in which so much – even (or especially) a marriage – depends not on love but on money. Austen is perhaps particularly satirising men here: while they may have money and power in her society, it is women who can, however indirectly, influence what men will do with their power – at least in human relationships.

Jane Austen's *Pride and Prejudice*

As in Austen's other novels – such as *Sense and Sensibility* (1811), *Mansfield Park* (1814) and *Emma* (1816) – we are presented in *Pride and Prejudice* with a number of possible and actual marriages. Early in the book, we learn that a pompous and foolish vicar, Mr Collins, is – as Mr Bennet's nearest male relative – destined to inherit Mr Bennet's money. When Mr Collins proposes to the Bennet's second daughter, Elizabeth, her mother, a silly and ignorant woman, urges her to agree, but Elizabeth refuses, with her father's approval. In Mr and Mrs Bennet's marriage we see two unworthy characters, although at first we may think that Austen is criticising only the selfish and easily flustered Mrs Bennet. Mrs Bennet's support of Elizabeth's marriage to Mr Collins is not so ridiculous as it might at first seem: while Mr Collins and Elizabeth have nothing in common and while Elizabeth finds Mr Collins' character repulsive, marriage to Mr Collins would bring her and her family financial security and allow her a measure of freedom. When Elizabeth's rather plain older friend Charlotte decides that Mr Collins is her best hope for creating a life in any degree her own, we are shown a marriage which not only works financially but gives the woman a freedom otherwise impossible for her. In contrast, Austen shows us at the end of this novel a marriage whose basis is impulsive passion in the relationship of Lydia Bennet and the rake George Wickham – such a union, we must feel, serves these superficial characters right, and Austen makes clear that both partners are too materialistic and immature to be happy with one another for very long.

Pride and Prejudice also presents us with three admirable marriages: between Jane Bennet and Charles Bingley; between Mr and Mrs Gardiner, the Bennet sisters' aunt and uncle; and between the novel's two central characters, Elizabeth and Fitzwilliam Darcy. Jane and Bingley seem to deserve one another, since both are reserved and morally worthy characters, mild in temperament, well-intentioned and kind. Despite misunderstandings not really of their own making, they marry at the end of the novel in a way that resolves problems and seems satisfying all round. Indeed, it is Bingley's 'fortune' that Austen refers to in her book's opening sentence, and it seems only fitting that Jane, the eldest daughter in the Bennet family, should marry the wealthy visitor, a union that her foolish mother not entirely foolishly set about to arrange from the beginning.

Mr and Mrs Gardiner are minor characters in the novel, but important figures nonetheless. Mrs Gardiner is Mrs Bennet's sister, and she has clearly made a better marriage than Mrs Bennet. Mrs Gardiner has married a good and wise man, who not only takes more responsibility for his family than Mr Bennet does, but manages – through middle-class commerce – to provide financially for them in ways Mr Bennet seems unable to do. Additionally, Mrs Gardiner seems happy in her relationship with her husband – unlike the Bennets, Mr and Mrs Gardiner appear to be personally well-suited to one another – and she has achieved a measure of independence in her society: she manages a household in London, reads widely, and has the freedom to travel.

Finally, Elizabeth and Darcy are presented as right for each other not because they fall in love at first sight – the author makes clear that just the opposite is true – but because they are similar in character and grow to care for one another, because each learns to moderate an initial 'pride' and early 'prejudices'. That both characters are finally drawn to one another erotically adds compelling dramatic tension to the narrative, but Austen never lets us forget that Darcy has 'a fortune', more money than Mr Bennet or Mr Collins or Charles Bingley; indeed, Darcy even has a family estate and a title. In other words, the marriage between Elizabeth and Darcy has all it needs to succeed within early 19th-century English society, and we are led to believe that it will make Elizabeth happy while allowing her – ironically – much of what her friend Charlotte also achieves through marriage: escape from the parental household and freedoms otherwise impossible for a woman.

The sentimental tradition

Not all women writers during the 19th or any other century used their work to express their serious engagement with the problematic issues of their time. Many popular authors voiced an unquestioning affirmation of conventional attitudes. Just as today Mills and Boon 'blouse-busters' and the American Harlequin Romance series continue to find a wide audience of readers interested in a diverting but predictable fantasy, so in the 19th century popular writers such as the British poet Felicia Hemans (1793–1835) found a wide audience eager for the sentimental treatment of a traditional topic. Consider, for instance, the final stanza of 'The Child's Last Sleep' (1828), Hemans' passionate response to a tomb decorated with a sculpted child and a butterfly:

> Thou'rt gone from us, bright one! – that *thou* shouldst die,
> And life be left to the butterfly!
> Thou'rt gone, as a dew-drop is swept from the bough –
> Oh! for the world where thy home is now!
> How may we love but in doubt and fear,
> How may we anchor our fond hearts here,
> How should e'en joy but a trembler be,
> Beautiful dust! when we look on thee?

▶ What literary devices does Hemans use here to solicit the reader's sympathy for her subject? Look at her punctuation, for instance, and her use of rhyme, regular metre, and diction. What does this poem gain – or lose – through her directly addressing the dead child? Hemans sentimentalises her subject through her use of **euphemisms** – such as 'gone' or 'where thy home is now'– and by calling the dead child 'Beautiful dust', making her feelings, although certainly sincere, seem excessive and, to the modern reader, even maudlin. How do you respond to her explicit expression of her theme in the poem's last four lines?

During a period of conventional Christian piety and high infant mortality, a poem on a dead child could be sure of finding responsive readers. Deserted by her husband, Hemans – like Aphra Behn a century earlier – managed to support herself and her five children through her writing. She was widely praised both during her lifetime and after her death, probably from the effects of rheumatic fever, at the age of 41. Indeed, collections of her verse appeared frequently until the 1920s. Although we may no longer admire her writing on aesthetic grounds, we can recognise her work as both an important reflection of the values of her age and evidence of the kind of writing women were encouraged to produce. Frederic Rowton's 1853 estimate of her achievement (an excerpt of which appears in Part 3, page 88) tells us as much about what contemporary readers expected of women writers as about Hemans herself.

Dorothy Wordsworth

In contrast to Hemans, many women writers have historically not even attempted to sell their work for money, writing instead for a private audience or even only for themselves. Dorothy Wordsworth (1771–1855) is best known as the Romantic poet

William Wordsworth's sister. Several of his poems (such as 'Lines composed a few miles above Tintern Abbey', 1798) mention her as a kindred spirit, and she shared a household with him even after he married her best friend, Mary Hutchinson. Dorothy Wordsworth travelled to Germany with her brother and their friend and fellow Romantic, the poet Samuel Taylor Coleridge, and her perceptions, as reflected in the journals she began in 1795, influenced their ideas and their work. Her unusually close relationship with her brother continued until her death, although both physical and mental ill health incapacitated her for the last 20 years of her life.

While Dorothy Wordsworth did not think of herself as an author, her journals, published only after her death, reveal her awareness of poetic techniques and the possibilities of language. She was especially responsive to sensory details, and her descriptions are vivid with colour, sound and texture. Consider, for example, this passage from *The Grasmere Journals*, written on 15 April 1802, recounting the experience of seeing daffodils while walking with her brother near Lake Windemere:

> When we were in the woods beyond Gowbarrow park we saw a few daffodils close to the water side, we fancied that the lake had floated the seeds ashore & that the little colony had so sprung up — But as we went along there were more & yet more & at last under the boughs of the trees, we saw that there was a long belt of them along the shore, about the breadth of a country turnpike road. I never saw daffodils so beautiful they grew among the mossy stones about & about them, some rested their heads upon these stones as on a pillow for weariness & the rest tossed & reeled & danced, & seemed as if they verily laughed with the wind that blew upon them over the Lake, they looked so gay ever glancing ever changing.

Five years later, her brother published his response to the same scene in 'The Daffodils' (1807). Compare the poem's opening lines with Dorothy Wordsworth's journal entry:

> I wandered lonely as a cloud
> That floats on high o'er vales and hills,
> When all at once I saw a crowd,
> A host, of golden daffodils;
> Beside the lake, beneath the trees,
> Fluttering and dancing in the breeze.

Later in this poem William Wordsworth describes the daffodils as stretching 'in a never-ending line/ Along the margin of a bay'; he says, 'Ten thousand saw I at a glance,/ Tossing their heads in sprightly dance.'

▶ What similarities do you notice between the journal entry and the poem? What words does the male poet literally borrow from his sister? What similar figures of speech does he use?

Interestingly, Dorothy Wordsworth emphasises the first-person plural, 'we', in her description, whereas her brother uses the first-person singular, 'I', throughout. It is worth asking what difference this makes. Her description of the daffodils near the lake concludes 'We rested again & again. The Bays were stormy, & we heard the waves at different distances & in the middle of the water like the sea.' In contrast, 'Daffodils' ends more philosophically. William Wordsworth asserts that 'A poet could not but be gay,/ In such a jocund company' of flowers, but when far away from the experience, the speaker, 'in vacant or in pensive mood', realises that the daffodils comfort him as both memory and inspiration:

> They flash upon that inward eye
> Which is the bliss of solitude;
> And then my heart with pleasure fills,
> And dances with the daffodils.

William Wordsworth defined poetry in a statement that has become famous: 'Poetry is emotion recollected in tranquillity.' Because she is writing a journal, however, Dorothy Wordsworth stresses the immediacy of events; she seldom thinks back upon them nor does she, because of her choice of genre, return to experiences to rework them into poems. Not all 19th-century women writers would be content to remain in the background, but it is possible to understand Dorothy Wordsworth's acceptance of a more traditional role in part as a response to being so much a part of the literary world of her brother and his friends. Many women found in their brothers or husbands alter-egos, as it were, for their own literary accomplishments, and felt fulfilled up to a point by the achievements of others at the cost of their own independent efforts. Other women – such as H.D., who married the English writer Richard Aldington, or the American poet Laura Riding (1901–1991), the English poet Robert Graves' partner for many years, or Sylvia Plath, who married the English poet Ted Hughes – would see their male partners in varying degrees as both colleagues and competitors. However, in the cases of all these women, as for Dorothy Wordsworth, the writing by the individual men in their lives provides an important context for understanding their own work, while the women's writing, in turn, provides an often overlooked context for understanding what their brothers and husbands wrote.

The Brontës

Other 19th-century women writers found themselves isolated from the mainstream of active literary life in a variety of ways. Charlotte Brontë, for example, lived far from London, the hub of English literary life in the 19th century as it remains today. Born in 1816, she lived most of her life in Haworth in rural Yorkshire, one of five daughters and one son of the local vicar, the authoritarian Patrick Brontë. Her mother died when Charlotte was five; her two older sisters died when she was nine. After periods at boarding school, Charlotte and her two surviving sisters, Emily (1818–1848) and Anne (1820–1849), took various teaching posts both in England and in Brussels, but in 1846, they chose the pseudonyms of Currer, Ellis and Acton Bell and began to publish their literary work.

Pen names

The Brontës' choice of pen names is interesting on several counts, both for what these pseudonyms hide and for what they reveal. Most obviously, these names hide the Brontës' identities as women; indeed, their editor at first thought they were men. 'Currer', 'Ellis' and 'Acton' are not, of course, in fact male names: they are made-up words, which sound like surnames, perhaps, but do not actually indicate gender; they are 'gender free'. Thus the young women first appeared as authors who, while not explicitly pretending to be men, left the interpretation of their gender to their readers. This pretence was possible in large measure because they did not live in London and were personally unknown in literary circles; thus the women turned what was in most ways a disadvantage into an advantage. The pen names also hid other personal details, including their family and their relative youth, giving the women the freedom of anonymity.

But the pseudonyms were also revealing. The three sisters chose the same surname, 'Bell', which identified them as relatives (their editor and early readers assumed they were brothers). The choice of a surname beginning with 'B' also echoed their real surname, thus becoming a sort of 'in joke', as were their first names, each of which began with the same letter as their real first names. Clearly, all three writers were aware of the unusual liberty writing allowed women of their time, and their word play suggests that they also understood from the very beginning of their literary careers the repressive system that privileged men. Additionally and importantly, their use of pen names allowed the women the freedom to use their own life experiences in their work, to both hide and reveal their personal histories, which they carefully selected and shaped and changed and even transformed for the purposes of effective fiction.

The Brontës' first book was a collection of their poems, but in 1847 each writer published her own individual and very different volume of fiction. Interestingly, these novels – Emily's *Wuthering Heights*, Anne's *Agnes Grey* and Charlotte's *Jane*

Eyre – all appeared under their useful pseudonyms. It was not until they had established themselves as published authors, praised by the literary establishment, that they decided to publish under their own names as women.

Wuthering Heights uses sophisticated narrative techniques, combining both the account of an unreliable upper-class male narrator, who is an outsider to the experiences he relates, and the version of events observed by a privileged female insider, the housekeeper Nellie Dean. The novel focuses on the forbidden passion between Catherine Earnshaw and her adopted brother Heathcliff, a wild and mysterious figure, who is both her secret lover and her alter-ego. Emily died of tuberculosis in 1848, the same year that Anne published her second book, *The Tenant of Wildfell Hall*. This novel, like *Agnes Grey*, draws on Anne's experience as a governess in an unhappy family, and offers a daring depiction of a woman who leaves her violent and drunken husband. Challenging Victorian social codes as well as the law, Helen Huntingdon takes their son with her and supports herself and him by her painting. Like Emily, Anne died of tuberculosis, at the age of 28 in 1849.

All of the novels by the Brontë sisters suggest the women's understanding of the dynamics of male power. This was something they learned about not only through their experience in schools and as governesses in others' families, but at home, where their father was a strong and often tyrannical figure, while their brother Branwell, their parents' favourite, was indulged throughout his life – a dissolute gambler and failed artist, he died in 1848 at the age of 31, his health weakened by alcoholism and drug addiction.

Jane Eyre

Charlotte Brontë's accomplished second novel, *Villette* (1853), draws on her experiences teaching at a girls' school in Brussels and her relationship with the school's principal, a married man; an earlier book, based on the same experiences and entitled *The Professor*, was only published in 1857, three years after Charlotte's death. But it was *Jane Eyre*, her best-known novel, that established her reputation as an accomplished writer.

The title character, a reliable and sympathetic first-person narrator, tells us the story of her life in five sections, each associated with a different stage and place in her development. The early parts of the book reveal the author's powerful portrayal of a blighted girlhood, and vividly convey the psychology of a lonely child. Limited in her experience of the world but aware of her own passionate nature and religious convictions, Jane has become a plain but spirited and intelligent young woman by the time she leaves school to assume a position at Thornfield as a governess to Adèle, Edward Fairfax Rochester's illegitimate daughter.

The love between Jane Eyre and her employer develops quickly, and is fuelled not only by their passionate personalities but by their clever conversation and the inequality in their status. Consider, for example, the following scene from Chapter 23. For several weeks, Rochester has teased Jane by suggesting that he loves another woman, Blanche Ingram. He begins apparently innocently, '"Thornfield is a pleasant place, is it not?... You must have become in some degree attached to the house …?"' When Jane admits that she is indeed attached to the house and to Adèle, Rochester leads her on, "'And would be sorry to part with them?'" Then:

> 'Pity!' he said, and sighed and paused. 'It is always the way of events in this life,' he continued presently: 'no sooner have you got settled in a pleasant resting-place, than a voice calls out to you to rise and move on, for the hour of repose is expired.'
>   'Must I move on, sir?' I asked. 'Must I leave Thornfield?'
>   'I believe you must, Jane. I am sorry, Janet, but I believe indeed you must.'

When Jane asks him outright if he is indeed going to be married, he responds, "'Ex-act-ly – Pre-cise-ly: with your usual acuteness, you have hit the nail straight on the head ... In about a month I hope to be a bridegroom, ... and in the interim, I myself shall look out for employment and an asylum for you."' Rochester even goes so far as to suggest "'a place I think will suit: it is to undertake the education of the five daughters of Mrs Dionysius O'Gall of Bitternut Lodge, Connaught, Ireland."' Jane responds:

> 'It is a long way off, sir.'
>   'No matter – a girl of your sense will not object to the voyage or the distance.'
>   'Not the voyage, but the distance: and then the sea is a barrier –'
>   'From what, Jane?'
>   'From England and from Thornfield: and –'
>   'Well?'
>   'From *you*, sir.'

Jane can contain herself no longer here and bursts into tears. Rochester continues to tease her, implying he will marry Miss Ingram. Jane then declares that, despite her enjoyment of his company, of talking 'face to face, with what I reverence, what I delight in – an original, a vigorous, an expanded mind', she must nevertheless leave. Rochester immediately insists that Jane must stay, but:

> 'I tell you I must go!' I retorted, roused to something like passion.
>   'Do you think I can stay to become nothing to you? Do you think I am an automaton? – a machine without feelings? and can bear to have my morsel of bread snatched from my lips, and my drop of living

water dashed from my cup? Do you think, because I am poor, obscure, plain, and little, I am soulless and heartless? You think wrong! – I have as much soul as you, – and full as much heart! And if God had gifted me with some beauty and much wealth, I should have made it as hard for you to leave me, as it is now for me to leave you. I am not talking to you now through the medium of custom, conventionalities, nor even of mortal flesh – it is my spirit that addresses your spirit; just as if both had passed through the grave, and we stood at God's feet, equal, – as we are!'

Throughout this passage, Rochester takes advantage of his more powerful position in the relationship.

▶ What devices does Brontë use to reveal the inequalities between these two characters? Look, for example, at how Rochester refers to Jane: as 'Jane', as 'Janet' (an affectionate diminutive), as 'a girl'. What does Jane call Rochester? What evidence do you find here of important differences in the two characters, in their levels of honesty and seriousness as well as in the degree of respect they show to each other? Consider Rochester's references to Jane's 'usual acuteness' and 'sense': what do you make of Rochester's use of flattery? Why do you suppose Rochester suggests that Jane go to Mrs O'Gall at Bitternut Lodge in Connaught, a very rural and rather bleak part of Ireland? What evidence do we have that he has made up this person? Why does Jane take him seriously?

Further, both characters here are aware that Jane is penniless while Rochester is wealthy; Jane is a servant while Rochester is her master. Jane's ethical and unselfish behaviour in the novel contrasts with Rochester's egocentric and manipulative treatment of her and the other women in his life; Rochester is a liar and a womaniser, while Jane strives to be truthful and pure. Jane may have the moral upper hand in their relationship, yet this seldom counts for much since for most of the book Rochester knows more than Jane does – about sex, about his own past – and the balance of power is thus often tipped in Rochester's favour.

This see-sawing of power relations makes Jane's and Rochester's love both erotic and dangerous, more to her than to him, but also for us, Brontë's readers. Do we really want her to reject such an attractive, witty and passionate man? Yet at what cost can she accept his advances or even his offer of marriage? Not only has Rochester fathered an illegitimate child, he left her mother alone and inadequately provided for in Belgium. Worse, it turns out that he already has a wife, the mad Bertha, a woman whom he portrays as possessed, whose marriage to him was a mistake from the start. But can we believe him? Can Jane? When Jane discovers Bertha's identity and refuses to marry Rochester, he offers her the alternative of becoming his mistress and moving with him to another country. Jane can only force herself to leave Rochester at this point, for she is being totally honest with him in her outburst in Chapter 23.

▶ Look again at Jane's long speech here. What evidence do we have in this passage that in this novel Brontë is challenging the attitudes (the customs and 'conventionalities') of her own time?

When *Jane Eyre* was published, it attained immediate popularity, but various critics objected to what they saw as the book's immorality. In her preface to the second edition, Brontë defended herself by asserting, 'Conventionality is not morality. Self-righteousness is not religion. To attack the first is not to assail the last.' Her position nevertheless placed her in opposition to her society in many ways, as she challenged her readers to rethink accepted ideas about the relationship between men and women.

Emily Dickinson

Another women writer who experienced some of the same isolation as the Brontës was the American poet Emily Dickinson (1830–1886), but Dickinson's response to her situation was quite different. Her father, like Patrick Brontë, was a dominant force in the family, which included her older brother Austin and her younger sister Lavinia as well as her rather weak and deferential mother. Like the Brontës, Dickinson lived far from the centres of literary activity of her day. Like Charlotte, Emily and Anne, Emily Dickinson came to know her natural surroundings very well and spent a great deal of her girlhood in the company of her family and other girls and young women.

Dickinson's father, however, was aware of the limitations imposed by his rural isolation in Amherst, a small university town in western Massachusetts. Trained as a lawyer, Mr Dickinson served for a few years in the state legislature 150 miles away in Boston and in the national legislature in Washington, D.C., where his family visited him. He encouraged his literary daughter's interests, and allowed her to use his large library. There she encountered a range of authors so important to her that she hung pictures of her favourites on her bedroom walls, prominent among them three very different British writers: the essayist Thomas Carlyle (1795–1881), the novelist George Eliot, and the poet Elizabeth Barrett Browning (1806–1861).

▶ Dickinson's favourite authors suggest her interest not only in a wide variety of genres in both the male and female literary traditions, but also a search for 'role models' that was at least as important to 19th-century women writers as to those who popularised the term in the 20th century. Look, for instance, at Elizabeth Barrett Browning's 'To George Sand' on page 87 in Part 3. Here Barrett Browning reveals her admiration for the French novelist George Sand (the pen name for Amandine Aurore Lucile, Baronne Dudevant, 1804–1876), known for her unconventional life (which included wearing men's clothing) and for her numerous love affairs. What qualities does Barrett Browning emphasise in her portrait of Sand? What is gained by the poet's depiction of Sand as a gladiator, fighting against 'lions' in a Roman 'circus'? What do Barrett Browning's tone and word choice reveal about her own values? On the basis of this sonnet, what do you feel might have made Barrett Browning particularly appealing to Dickinson?

Throughout her father's life, Dickinson read to him regularly from the local newspapers, becoming aware of much that was going on in the world and in all walks of life. Such an activity, especially during the years of the American Civil War (1861–1865), brought Dickinson into contact with experiences beyond her own limited daily life in Amherst. Poem 185, for instance, written in 1860, offers evidence of Dickinson's critical mind and sense of humour as well as her awareness of contemporary interest in science:

> 'Faith' is a fine invention
> When Gentlemen can *see* –
> But *Microscopes* are prudent
> In an Emergency.

Mr Dickinson believed in education for both girls and boys, and Emily attended the local schools and then Mount Holyoke Seminary, not a religious institution but the forerunner of the prestigious women's university now known as Mount Holyoke College. She stayed there for only a year, however, preferring the independence she enjoyed at home.

Conventionally religious, her community and family expected a degree of Protestant piety and church attendance, but Dickinson resisted such conformity. While at the seminary, Dickinson's classmates participated actively in church life, and most claimed an emotionally intense 'conversion experience', a personal affirmation of faith. Dickinson could not then nor later in her life respond with the public act of confession her church required, nor was she ever completely certain about her own salvation or even belief in God. Her poetry offers evidence of her changing moods, for sometimes she felt sure of God and His goodness, while at other times throughout her life she questioned His nature and even His existence. For instance, she reflects on the possibility of an afterlife in poem 101, asking, 'Will there really be a "Morning"?/ Is there such a thing as "Day"?' (Part 3, pages 88–89). Her doubt of the Christian concept of heaven is also clear in poem 243, written in 1861:

I've known a Heaven, like a Tent –
To wrap its shining Yards –
Pluck up its stakes, and disappear –
Without the sound of Boards
Or Rip of Nail – Or Carpenter –
But just the miles of Stare –
That signalize a Show's Retreat –
In North America –

No Trace – no Figment of the Thing
That dazzled, Yesterday,
No Ring – no Marvel –
Men, and Feats –
Dissolved as utterly –
As Bird's far Navigation
Discloses just a Hue –
A plash of Oars, a Gaiety –
Then swallowed up, of View.

▶ How is the speaker's concept of heaven here like a circus tent in small-town America in the 19th century? What evidence do we have in this poem that the speaker is uneasy, shocked or even bitter at what she presents as her earlier delusions about heaven's existence?

At other times, Dickinson could confidently assert her belief in God and traditional Christian teachings about life after death. Consider poem 1052, written in 1865:

I never saw a Moor –
I never saw the Sea –
Yet know I how the Heather looks
And what a Billow be.

I never spoke with God
Nor visited in Heaven –
Yet certain am I of the spot
As if the Checks were given –

▶ What indications does the speaker here give of her limited experience? On what might she base her knowledge of heather, waves and heaven? 'Moor' is not a very American word, and to an American strongly evokes the geography of northern England; 'Moor' here even suggests that Dickinson has been reading the Brontës, copies of whose works we know were available in her father's library. Thus Dickinson hints that her knowledge of the world and perhaps of God as well comes from her wide reading. 'Checks' are the tokens given in at particular points on 19th-century railway lines so that no more than one train uses a specific track at any one time. What does poem 1052 gain from such a precise technical term?

Dickinson's confidence was not always so reassuring, however. Look at poem 338, written in 1862:

> I know that He exists.
> Somewhere – in Silence –
> He has hid his rare life
> From our gross eyes.
>
> 'Tis an instant's play.
> 'Tis a fond Ambush –
> Just to make Bliss
> Earn her own surprise!
>
> But – should the play
> Prove piercing earnest –
> Should the glee – glaze –
> In Death's – stiff – stare –
>
> Would not the fun
> Look too expensive!
> Would not the jest –
> Have crawled too far!

While Dickinson begins this poem by asserting, 'I know that He exists', the first stanza continues with unnerving lines: 'Somewhere – in Silence –/ He has hid his rare life/ From our gross eyes.' The poem concludes that God may be cruelly playing with us; there may be no 'Bliss' after death, indeed no afterlife at all.

Dickinson remained at home in her father's house for the rest of her life. Her brother married her best friend and moved into a large residence next door; Lavinia remained at home to keep house for Emily, and Dickinson herself never married, apparently by her own choice. She was witty, vivacious and attractive, but she was also eccentric, intense, and definite about her feelings and convictions. Beginning in her twenties, she withdrew more and more from society and increasingly defined herself by her writing: she maintained an extensive correspondence with a number of male and female friends and acquaintances, devoting much of her time to reading and especially to her own poetry. She insisted on dressing in white, refusing to attend church and refusing eventually to leave her house. By the end of her life, she even refused to receive visitors.

After Dickinson's death, her sister and sister-in-law were shocked to discover nearly 2,000 poems neatly stored in a trunk in her room. Reluctant to destroy what was clearly so important to her, they preserved them, publishing a selection in 1890, followed by other volumes. Only seven of Dickinson's poems had been published in her lifetime, and contemporary editors – more used to poetry such as that written by Felicia Hemans – regularised Dickinson's punctuation and changed words and phrasing in order to make the metre more even and the diction more conventional. Further, her editors added titles and often grouped the poems in thematic sections with simplistic or trivialising headings such as 'Happiness' or 'Spring' or 'Death' or 'Birds'.

Until the middle of the 20th century only a fraction of Dickinson's work had made it into print, and all of the poems were selected and edited to make their form (**free verse** stanzas with **slant rhyme** and frequent dashes) and content more traditional. It was only in 1955 that Thomas H. Johnson produced for the first time an edition of 1,775 of Dickinson's poems (all of the poems he could then find in the archive at Amherst College). As closely as he was able, he reproduced Dickinson's distinctive punctuation and the words exactly as she had written them; he also arranged the poems chronologically, dating them as carefully as he could. Perhaps in part because Dickinson chose not to publish her work, she did not give her poems individual titles, and they are properly referred to now by their first lines or by the numbers Johnson assigned to them.

Although she seems to have been absolutely convinced of her literary gifts and confident that her poetry was an important literary achievement, it is perhaps no wonder that Dickinson herself chose not to seek publication for most of her work.

▶ Consider poem 288 (Part 3, page 89). What does the poet mean by the terms 'Nobody' and 'Somebody'? The tone of this poem may be light and humorous, but what evidence can you find here that Dickinson is also satirising the literary standards of her day? Contrast poem 288 with the more serious poem 441 (Part 3, page 91). To what does the initial pronoun 'This' refer? Why do you suppose that the speaker here refers to her readers as 'Sweet – countrymen'? You might also look carefully at some of her other poems about poetry, for instance poem 308 (Part 3, page 90).

Dickinson was well aware of the consequences of her choices. By not publishing, she risked anonymity but gained an autonomy over her writing. By not marrying, she was rejecting woman's traditional role of wife and mother, even explicitly questioning the advantages of such conventional behaviour in her society. Consider poem 199, written in 1860:

I'm 'wife '– I've finished that –
That other state –
I'm Czar – I'm 'Woman' now –
It's safer so –

How odd the Girl's life looks
Behind this soft Eclipse –
I think that Earth feels so
To folks in Heaven – now –

This being comfort – then
That other kind – was pain –
But why compare?
I'm 'Wife'! Stop there!

▶ In these stanzas, the poet assumes the voice of a married woman in order to suggest the repressive strictures that wives of her time were forced to endure. In the first line, the speaker asserts her title as 'wife', apparently content with her state. But is she really? What evidence do we have in the poem that the speaker has doubts about the privileges supposedly enjoyed by a married woman? What does Dickinson suggest by calling marriage 'this soft Eclipse'? The poem is enriched by the comparison between marriage and heaven in the second stanza; what do you make of the speaker's reluctance to develop the comparison in stanza three? You might pay particular attention in your reading of this poem to Dickinson's punctuation: look at her use of inverted commas, capitalisation, dashes and exclamation marks. How do these distinctive indicators of tone help to reveal the speaker's character and Dickinson's point of view?

In 'The Soul selects her own Society –' (poem 303 in Part 3, pages 89–90), Dickinson presents her solitude as a conscious choice with serious consequences. Having made her decision, she must then steel herself to resist all other options. Note how in this poem the author emphasises the speaker's power as well as her gender.

▶ Do you think the situation Dickinson presents in poem 303 would be different for a male poet-speaker? Try changing all the feminine pronouns in the poem to masculine ones. What differences do these changes make?

For Dickinson, being a poet meant separating herself to a degree from the world and devoting herself to a life of the mind rather than to domestic responsibilities, a particular partner, marriage or motherhood. This unusual choice did not mean, however, that she was ignorant of erotic life nor that she rejected it. In poem 249 (Part

3, page 89), the poet begins with a powerful exclamation ('Wild Nights – Wild Nights!') and imagines that, if the speaker were with the lover whom the poem addresses, together 'Wild Nights should be/ Our luxury!' Specifically, as Dickinson indicates in poem 657 (Part 3, page 91), to be a poet meant dwelling 'in Possibility', living in 'Paradise' through emotional and intellectual engagement with her writing rather than literally seeking out sexual experience.

Dickinson knew that her choices and behaviour might be seen by some people as a form of madness. Indeed, the accusation of madness or even witchcraft has traditionally been used by those in power to discount women's abilities and achievements. Well aware that her contemporaries failed to understand her and her work, Dickinson explains her position explicitly in poem 435 (Part 3, page 90): while most people would have called her 'mad' or even 'dangerous', here she asserts triumphantly, 'Much Madness is divinest Sense –/ To a discerning Eye –'.

Women writers at the end of the 19th century

While the marriage plot continued to be important to writers throughout the 19th and 20th centuries, Emily Dickinson and other women of her period were clearly conscious that marriage raised as many problems for women as it apparently solved. Indeed, in both America and Britain, women were mobilising their energies and beginning to raise explicitly feminist issues in publically political ways. The 19th century was, after all, the age of Charles Darwin (1809–1882) and Karl Marx (1818–1883), and scientific and philosophical ideas were widely discussed not only in universities but in daily newspapers, not only in the mansions of the wealthy and educated, but in pubs and cafés and factories where working-class people congregated. In 1848, the year in which Marx published his *Communist Manifesto*, there were revolutions throughout Europe, while in the United States the first women's rights convention was held in Seneca Falls, New York. Social unrest and concern with social welfare became important political issues in the second half of the century.

In 1863 the American President Abraham Lincoln proclaimed the emancipation of slaves throughout the nation. The various groups which had focused on this subject now developed wider concerns involving the emancipation of oppressed people more generally, including those oppressed by poverty, ignorance and gender. Darwin's theory of 'the survival of the fittest' seemed to many people cruel and unjust when applied literally to social situations in which individuals were deprived, for example, of health care, education, and access to political power. When the English nurse Florence Nightingale (1820–1910) campaigned for better hygiene, she found an audience in part because she captured in her work the spirit of the time. In *Cassandra* (written in 1851 and 1852, but not published until 1928) – a work now seen as an important feminist text linking Wollstonecraft and Woolf – Nightingale argued that:

Passion, intellect, moral activity – these three have never been satisfied in a woman. In this cold and oppressive conventional atmosphere, they cannot be satisfied. To say more on this subject would be to enter into [an examination of] the whole of society, of the present state of civilisation.

Nightingale reflected: 'Widowhood, ill-health, or want of bread, these three explanations or excuses are supposed to justify a woman taking up an occupation. In some cases, no doubt, an indomitable force of character will suffice without any of these, but such are rare.' Nightingale was angered by what she saw as the waste of female talents:

Now, why is it more ridiculous for a man than for a woman to do worsted work [knitting] and drive out every day in a carriage?... Is man's time more valuable than woman's? or is the difference between man and woman this, that woman has confessedly nothing to do?

(from *Cassandra*, ed. Myra Stark 1978)

Nightingale's use of **rhetorical questions** here emphasises her point: society needs to change so that women can realise their potential. Indeed, women on both sides of the Atlantic found a common cause in their concern for social reform. Women's suffrage, first advocated by Mary Wollstonecraft in 1792, was opposed by Queen Victoria, but the idea now began to receive organised and increasingly vocal support.

Elizabeth Gaskell and Charlotte Perkins Gilman

A writer such as Emily Dickinson was temperamentally unsuited to public demonstrations and group effort, but she was certainly influenced by the issues of her age and they had a clear impact on her own views. Other writers were more direct in addressing the social problems of their time. For instance, Dickinson's English contemporary, Christina Rossetti (1830–1894), explored both the dangers and the sensual appeal of male seduction as well as the importance of friendship between sisters in her narrative poem 'Goblin Market' (1862), while Elizabeth Barrett Browning was an ardent feminist whose work included not only the verse novel *Aurora Lee* (1856), an account of her own artistic development, but poems of social protest on such subjects as Italian politics and child labour.

Charlotte Brontë's friend and biographer, the novelist Elizabeth Gaskell (1810–1865), and the American feminist Charlotte Perkins Gilman (1860–1935) also used their work to address social and political issues more explicitly. Gaskell's novels raised her readers' awareness of the exploitative conditions in which many women lived. In *Mary Barton: A Tale of Manchester Life* (1848), for instance, she analysed the experience of a working-class woman in northern England. In *North and South* (1855), she explored the relationships between workers and their masters. In *Ruth* (1853), she daringly depicted the experiences of a woman who is seduced and then bears an illegitimate child.

Charlotte Perkins Gilman's thinking resulted from rigorous intellectual social analysis. She called for women's economic independence in *Women and Economics* (1898), a manifesto subtitled *The Economic Relation between Men and Women as a Factor in Social Evolution*, in which she argued against contemporary romanticised notions of womanhood and motherhood while defining domestic chores and child-care as social and communal responsibilities. In her novel *Herland* (1915), Gilman went so far as to imagine a feminist utopia in which women existed happily in a world without men. In contrast, a writer like the American Kate Chopin (1851–1904) used her fiction to examine the experience of women denied the opportunities they needed to realise their own potential.

Kate Chopin

Born in the American Midwest, Chopin moved to Louisiana when she married Oscar Chopin, an American of French descent, at the age of 20. Her experience of life in this part of the American south had a profound effect on her, as she became aware of Creole, Cajun, black and native American cultures. When her husband died ten years later, she returned to Kentucky with her six children. Financially secure, she now had the leisure to develop her own interests and began to write. Her novels and stories, set in New Orleans or the surrounding Bayous, often feature characters with various racial and cultural backgrounds and directly address issues of sexual power, gender, social convention and female identity.

In her short story 'Désirée's Baby' (1894) , for example, Désirée and her husband are Creoles, French-Americans. When the young couple's baby turns out to have black skin, Désirée is held responsible and, despite her protests, her husband accuses her of adultery and leaves her. Chopin's stories, many of them quite brief, frequently depend on ironic plot twists. Can you anticipate what the husband discovers about his own family lineage at the end of 'Désirée's Baby'?

Chopin is also known for her frank treatment of sexuality. In another story, 'The Storm' (1900), Chopin recounts a meeting between Calixta and Alcée, who are both now married to other people. Calixta has a relatively happy marriage, while Alcée is rather estranged from his petty but affectionate wife. Caught in a heavy thunderstorm, Alcée seeks shelter at Calixta's house in the countryside. They rekindle the passion they have always felt for each other (which Chopin had depicted in an earlier tale, 'At the 'Cadian Ball', 1894), and they go to bed together. The torrential rain and wind outside Calixta's house parallel the two characters' feelings and actions, but Chopin gives her story an ironic twist: Alcée goes calmly back to the city with a more accepting attitude towards his wife, while Calixta is absolutely delighted when her husband and son return home safely. The narrative concludes, 'So the storm passed and everyone was happy.'

In 'The Story of an Hour' (1894), Chopin addresses explicitly the problems an oppressive marriage posed for a woman. When Louise Mallard is informed of her husband Brently's death in a train accident, she bursts into tears and retreats to her room. Despite what her relatives – and she herself – expect, after an initial moment of shock, Louise finds herself whispering, '"Free! Body and soul free!"' Chopin explains:

> She knew that she would weep again when she saw the kind, tender hands folded in death; the face that had never looked save with love upon her, fixed and gray and dead. But she saw beyond that bitter moment a long procession of years to come that would belong to her absolutely. And she opened and spread her arms out to them in welcome.

What ironies do you find here? What is gained by Chopin's statement that Brently had never looked upon Louise 'save with love'? What do you make of the fact that in this paragraph, as throughout this tale, the central characters are almost always referred to not by their names but by pronouns ('she' and 'her' here), and that Brently's hands and face are simply referred to as 'the kind, tender hands' and 'the face'? This story does not stop with Louise's sense of liberation, however. It turns out that Brently was in fact 'far from the scene of the accident', and when he returns home at his normal time, Louise faints. Chopin concludes succinctly, 'When the doctors came they said she had died of heart disease – of joy that kills.' What further ironies does Chopin's final sentence add to this story?

Chopin is best known for her novel *The Awakening* (1899), which tells the story of a woman who struggles to free herself from the conventions that define her, that repress her individual identity and work to keep her 'asleep'. Edna grows up in Kentucky, where she romantically dreams of marrying a dashing cavalry officer. Instead, she settles for the kind and ordinary Creole, Léonce Pontellier – Chopin calls their marriage 'an accident' – and moves to New Orleans, a cosmopolitan city where her life is influenced by the sophisticated local French culture. The narrative is set here and in the nearby seaside community of Grand Isle, where Edna, Léonce, and their two young sons spend their summer holidays. During the course of the novel, Edna becomes vaguely but deeply dissatisfied with her traditional married life, and cannot understand what is wrong. She tells Madame Ratignolle, her happily married friend who is joyfully pregnant with her fourth child, that although she loves her boys, she cannot define herself as what Chopin calls a 'mother-woman'. Edna confesses, 'I would give up the inessential; I would give my money, I would give my life for my children, but I wouldn't give myself.'

Madame Ratignolle represents one way of being a woman; another alternative is presented in the character of Mademoiselle Reisz, an older woman who has never married and devotes herself to music. Mademoiselle Reisz is a gifted pianist whose skills and discipline have been developed from childhood. When Edna tries to emulate this artist by taking up painting, an activity she enjoyed as a girl, her mediocre work fails to give her the fulfilment for which she longs. Unsettled and increasingly upset, Edna becomes distressed when her attraction to Robert Lebrun seems to have been for him merely a pleasant summer flirtation; her affair with Alcée Arobin, a dashing playboy, confirms her sexual awakening, but is not exactly or completely what she wants and needs. Having learned to swim during the summer, Edna returns to Grand Isle out of season. Chopin vividly portrays her distracted psychological state. Both in tune with the elemental water and her own physical nature, and out of tune with the repressive social attitudes of her time and place, Edna walks naked into the sea and drowns.

Contemporary readers were positively impressed by the power of Chopin's prose, but many were also shocked by the social criticism and sexual frankness of *The Awakening*. Indeed, the many harsh reviews undermined Chopin's confidence. Despite her rebellious views and insights into the position of women in late 19th-century America, Chopin published only seven more stories before her death from a sudden stroke in 1904.

▶ Some readers might find Chopin's work melodramatic; do you feel that her psychological insights and feminist concerns justify her dramatic plots and the intensity of emotion on which she concentrates? Look at the final paragraphs of *The Awakening* in Part 3, pages 92–93. What literary techniques does the author use to convey her character's perceptions? How does Chopin use sensory impressions and memory here? Edna's relation to the sea is both symbolic and sensual: what is gained by having her swim naked? How does Chopin use contrast in this passage to convey her themes?

The 20th century

When in 1974 Adrienne Rich looked back on the history of women's writing, she concluded in an essay on the American poet Anne Sexton that women had to fight against the temptation to commit suicide – whether literal suicide, like that of Chopin's Edna Pontellier, or figurative suicide, a silencing or muting of their own voices in response to society's expectations of what women ought to be. Indeed, there is an appalling tradition of female suicides, of women who, unwilling or unable to conform to the social pressures of their day, have destroyed themselves. Yet some readers have argued that suicide in cases such as Edna's can be understood as an assertive act, the only possibility left to a woman in particular circumstances. Suffering from breast cancer, the feminist writer Charlotte Perkins Gilman killed herself before she could become a burden to others. Virginia Woolf, despite all she wrote about the tragedy of Shakespeare's sister's death (see Part 3, pages 94–95), made a suicide pact with her Jewish husband, Leonard Woolf: if Germany invaded Britain during the Second World War, both agreed to kill themselves rather than endure Nazi persecution.

Indeed, Woolf feared the Second World War in part because of her experience of the First World War (1914–1918). For her, as she indicated in *A Room of One's Own*, the Great War was a major turning point in history.

▶ Look at 'The Manx Cat' in Part 3, pages 93–94. Why do you suppose Woolf uses the phrase 'before the war' three times in this passage? What does her quotation of the romantic, even sentimental lines by Alfred, Lord Tennyson suggest?

If, in our consideration of women's writing, we can understand the 19th century as beginning about the time of the French Revolution in 1789 – that is, with Wollstonecraft's *A Vindication of the Rights of Woman* in 1792 – then we can understand the end of this era as occurring with the First World War, a time when illusions were shattered for women and men throughout the world. It is not surprising, therefore, that women were formally given a political voice in the years immediately following the Armistice. For example, in Britain and most of Canada as well as in Germany, Austria and Russia, many (though not all) women were granted suffrage in 1918; women in America finally won the right to vote in 1920. Only in 1971, however, did women receive the vote in Switzerland, the same year in which the voting age for both women and men in the United States was lowered from 21 to 18, while black women – and black men – in South Africa were not granted the right to vote until 1994.

The vote and the limits of power

The 20th century saw women and men trying to come to terms with what this limited political power might – or might not – mean. Women in Britain could vote after 1918, but only if they were 30 years old or over. Not until 1928 – the year in which Woolf wrote *A Room of One's Own* – was the vote granted to British women on an equal basis with men. Although women had been attending British universities and completing degree requirements since the late 19th century, often with superior results, it was only in 1920 that Oxford decided to grant degrees to women for the first time, while at Cambridge, women would not be allowed to receive degrees until after the Second World War, in 1946.

Indeed, for women throughout the world what at first might have looked like the achievement of equal status with men, often proved not to be the case.

Women's professional opportunities during the century offer a good illustration of the attitudes women writers had to confront. Despite the changes brought about by the First World War, women in the first half of the 20th century, who had been receiving degrees in the United States since the late 1800s, had few career choices open to them. If they decided to teach, as many women did, they often found themselves teaching younger children – as is the case today in both Britain and America – and at a lower rate of pay than their male counterparts. If they decided to pursue careers in medicine, they were usually encouraged to become nurses rather than doctors.

In fact, in any career that women entered, they found themselves in lower-paid and lower-status positions relative to men. For instance, in the 19th century, when the typewriter was a new technological tool, men served, as they had for centuries, as secretaries to other men. When the typewriter came to be seen, like the telephone, as a commonplace device, women became secretaries in large numbers – and this office job remains one almost invariably filled by women. In turn, a secretary changed from being a sort of apprentice to a person in power to being, at least into the 1970s, a skilled servant whose job involved not only typing but such tasks as preparing and serving coffee to mostly male superiors. Until the 1960s, if a woman married, as most did, she was usually urged – and in many instances required – to give up her paid job. If she was allowed to remain in the work force, she generally had to leave once she became pregnant – and she usually did become pregnant.

Reproductive and sexual freedom remain issues for women throughout the world even into the 21st century. In many states in America, for example, condoms could not be freely purchased until the 1960s, while the birth control pill was not widely available until the 1970s. Even today birth control and abortion in many parts of the world are not affordable or even available options for many women, while the AIDS epidemic has also had an immense impact on women, limiting their sexual activity and endangering their lives and those of their children as well as the lives of their male relatives and friends.

Women's status and modern women writers

What is the impact on women writers of realities such as those just described? How have women writers responded to the contradictions and challenges of the modern age? These are exactly the questions Virginia Woolf addressed when she continued to develop the ideas she first wrote about explicitly in *A Room of One's Own*. In 1938, she published *Three Guineas*, a book about preventing war. Here, Woolf argued that the same social forces that work to disempower women also work to bring about war. She contended that only through the prevention of war and violence would women and other excluded groups ever have a chance to realise their potential, to live independent and fully realised lives. During the course of her career, Woolf became philosophically sophisticated and more and more aware of the unequal distribution of power. She used her writing to explore and extend her increasingly political ideas and convictions, and expressed herself in a wide range of genres; she produced, for example, voluminous diaries and thousands of letters as well as both fiction (such as her anti-war novel *Mrs Dalloway*, 1925), and essays.

In the late 1960s, the feminism we find in writers who campaigned for women's suffrage before the First World War resurfaced in the 'women's liberation' movement. Today's thinking about women's experience and specifically about women's writing is rooted in what is now called this 'second wave' of feminist thought. After 1920, other concerns – for example, poverty or war or race or class – captured the imaginations of most people who clamoured for political action. Unlike Virginia Woolf, many women failed to see that privilege of any sort created the hierarchies that excluded women from power and independence just as much as, for example, they excluded black people in the American south in the 1920s or Jews in Germany in the 1930s. In the 1940s and 1950s, even many intelligent and educated women seemed eager to embrace lives in which they were defined and limited by men.

▶ Consider Phyllis McGinley's poem, 'The 5:32' (Part 3, pages 97–98). Known for her humorous verse, popular essays and children's books, McGinley often wrote out of her own experience as a wife and mother raising her family in a comfortable post-war American suburb.

What sort of life does the speaker lead? What elements in this sonnet suggest contentment with a life dependent on a man? What is gained by McGinley's emphasis on the housewife as the speaker here? What hints are there of disturbing realities beyond the 'hour best of all the hours' the speaker knows? Are you attracted to the world described in the poem or could you accuse the speaker – or the poet – of complacency?

▶ Now consider 'Ode for Ted' (Part 3, pages 98–99), written a few years later by another American poet, Sylvia Plath. Usually remembered for her sharp wit, anger and bravado, as well as for the pain of her suicide in 1963, in this poem Plath seems to exult in her relationship to a man.

What attracts the speaker to 'Ted'? In what ways is the speaker defined by him? Are you disturbed by the passion the speaker feels for her lover? As fellow poets, Sylvia Plath and Ted Hughes strongly influenced each others' writing. On the basis of this poem, do you see 'Ted' as empowering or disempowering the speaker? To what degree does the speaker seem aware of the ironies of her situation?

'The Feminine Mystique'

The perception of ironies was often difficult for women to achieve. Employing techniques suggested by Lenin, and later by Mao (in the Little Red Book) for creating political awareness in those oppressed by elitist societies, the women's liberation movement used 'consciousness raising' in the 1960s and 1970s to help women to see their situation more clearly. As early as 1949, the French writer Simone de Beauvoir had examined women's disenfranchised position in her ground-breaking book *The Second Sex*. In 1963, the American feminist Betty Friedan published *The Feminine Mystique*, in which she began to define the sense of confusing emptiness experienced by many American women in the post-war period. In the late 1960s and early 1970s numerous books by women grappled with the nature of women's position in the modern world, among them Mary Ellmann's *Thinking about Women* (1968), Kate Millett's *Sexual Politics* (1969), Shulamith Firestone's *The Dialectic of Sex* (1970), and Germaine Greer's *The Female Eunuch* (1970).

Sylvia Plath

Plath's life ended before modern feminism made explicit many of the difficulties raised in her writing, but she came on her own to an awareness we can now understand as feminist. Born into a middle-class family in New England, Plath's father and mother were German immigrants. Otto Plath taught biology at Boston University; his speciality was bees. Plath's mother Aurelia taught secretarial skills. Both of her parents encouraged Plath to excel academically, and she was an outstanding student at school and at Smith College, an exclusive university for women. She began to write as a child, and before she was 20, her work appeared in popular journals. In the summer of 1953, she won a month's 'guest editorship' at the fashion magazine *Mademoiselle* in New York City, an experience she describes in her autobiographical novel *The Bell Jar* (1963).

The contradictions Plath confronted as a young adult precipitated a mental breakdown: Plath attempted to kill herself, and spent the following year in an institution where, among other therapies, she was given electro-shock treatments – experiences she describes in horrifying detail in her novel. Plath returned to Smith College in 1954, graduating with high honours in 1955. With the support of a Fulbright Fellowship, she studied at Cambridge University for two years, where in 1956 she met and soon after married Ted Hughes. A published poet, Hughes impressed Plath; he was, she wrote to her mother, the only man she had ever met who was 'big enough for me'. After a brief period in the United States, they moved to London and then to Devon. Their children, a girl and a boy, were born in 1960 and 1962.

Plath was intensely competitive, and her husband's literary ambitions and achievements both inspired and threatened her own writing. Hughes' infidelities with other women infuriated her, while her intense and volatile personality made a settled married life impossible. Hughes left Plath in the autumn of 1962. Having returned to London during the coldest winter for decades, Plath killed herself on 11 February 1963: depressed and anxious, unable to sleep and writing through the nights at a furious rate the best poetry of her short career, Plath carefully provided mugs of milk for her small children, then sealed the door to the kitchen of her flat and put her head in the gas oven.

Plath's letters and journals

Plath's letters and journals document not only the contradictions she experienced, but her distress at her inability to resolve them. Her correspondence with her mother, published as *Letters Home* in 1975, poignantly reveals the tensions on which Plath drew in her poetry. For instance, in 1949, at the age of 17, she wrote to her mother:

> I am afraid of getting married. Spare me from cooking three meals a day – spare me from the relentless cage of routine and rote. I want to be free ... Yet if I were not in this body, where *would* I be – perhaps I am *destined* to be classified and qualified. But, oh, I cry out against it. I am I – I am powerful – but to what extent? I am I.
>
> (from *Letters Home: Correspondence 1950–1963*, ed. Aurelia Schober Plath, 1975)

In contrast, in early 1956 Plath wrote in her journal, 'My God, I'd love to cook and make a house, and surge force into a man's dreams ...'. A year later Plath reflected, 'All my pat theories against marrying a writer dissolve with Ted: his rejections [from publishers] more than double my sorrow & his acceptances rejoice me more than mine – it is as if he is the perfect male counterpart to my own self ...'.

Working on a novel that would eventually become *The Bell Jar*, Plath revealed in 1957 a sophisticated awareness of the tradition of women's literary expression, acknowledging that 'Virginia Woolf helps. Her novels make mine possible.' Plath admired Woolf's non-fiction as well, for she indicates in this journal entry that the protagonist of *The Bell Jar*, Esther Greenwood, was initially called 'Judith Greenwood', recalling Woolf's Judith Shakespeare. Yet Plath was also repeatedly drawn towards male models, whom she idealised – for instance, D.H. Lawrence, James Joyce, W.B. Yeats and Dylan Thomas. As her marriage to Ted Hughes became increasingly rocky, Plath confessed in her journal in late 1958, 'I must be happy first in my own work and struggle to that end, so my life does not hang on Ted's.' In early 1959, Plath wrote even more specifically about the contradictions she found increasingly constraining:

I have hated men because I felt them physically necessary: hated them because they would degrade me, by their attitude: women shouldn't think, shouldn't be unfaithful (but their husbands may be), must stay home, cook, wash. Many men need a woman to be like this. Only the weak ones don't, so many strong women marry a weak one, to have children, and their own way at once. If I could once see how to write a story, a novel, to get something of my feeling over, I would not despair. If writing is not an outlet, what is?

(from *The Journals of Sylvia Plath*, ed. Ted Hughes and Frances McCullough, 1982)

By the last months of her life, Plath seems to have come to a deeper if acutely painful understanding of both herself and her work. She wrote to her mother on 16 October 1962, 'I am a genius of a writer; I have it in me. I am writing the best poems of my life; they will make my name ...'. Plath's exuberance here seems justified by the extraordinary power of her late verse, yet even her well-founded confidence was invariably and ironically undercut by the severe depression that drove her to suicide. On her last birthday (27 October 1962), Plath wrote 'Poppies in October', a poem that poignantly captures the tensions and ironies of both her life and her best work:

Even the sun-clouds this morning cannot manage such skirts.
Nor the woman in the ambulance
Whose red heart blooms through her coat so astoundingly—

A gift, a love gift
Utterly unasked for
By a sky

Palely and flamily
Igniting its carbon monoxides, by eyes
Dulled to a halt under bowlers.

Oh my God, what am I
That these late mouths should cry open
In a forest of frost, in a dawn of cornflowers.

▶ What contrasts do you notice in this poem? Consider the colours Plath mentions or suggests; consider as well the contrast between the first stanza (with its female images) and the third stanza (whose images are masculine). Do the images in this poem startle you? What is the effect of the poet's introduction of 'I' in the poem's last stanza? And what is the 'gift' that Plath refers to in line four?

Carol Ann Duffy

Carol Ann Duffy's work offers a stark contrast to Sylvia Plath's writing. Born in Glasgow in 1955, Duffy grew up in Staffordshire, where she attended a convent school and a girls' grammar school; she then went on to read philosophy at the University of Liverpool. From a less privileged background than Plath, Duffy came of age in a markedly different time and place. Encouraged to write by her teachers and by the Liverpool poet Adrian Henri (with whom she began a relationship when she was 16 and he 39), Duffy was also empowered by the feminism of the 1970s, and has led a life both more public and more private than Plath's. While it has never been easy to establish a career as a writer or to earn one's living by writing, Duffy has been generously supported by prizes and grants since 1982. Her dramatic works have been broadcast on BBC radio and performed on the London stage, and from her very first volume of verse, *Standing Female Nude* (1985), her work has received excellent reviews and achieved a comparatively wide readership.

This recognition is in line with what Duffy has seen as her public role and even obligation as a writer. For instance, throughout her career she has been committed to bringing literature to young people and to readers from all social backgrounds. She worked officially as a writer in East London schools for two years in the early 1980s, and has recently written several books for children (among them *Rumpelstiltskin and Other Grimm Tales* in 1999 and *Queen Munch and Queen Nibble* in 2002). She has also written numerous poems set in schools, which concern themselves with experiences young people can share.

'The Laughter of Stafford Girls' High'

In Duffy's *Feminine Gospels* (2002) the long narrative poem 'The Laughter of Stafford Girls' High' begins with a note passed surreptitiously in a geography class: Carolann Clare (whose name, of course, suggests the author's) 'passed a note, which has never been found, / to the classmate in front, Emily Jane, a girl/ who adored the teacher ...'. The unsuppressable and contagious laughter which results disrupts not only this class but the entire school, eventually causing it to shut down completely:

> The empty school creaked and sighed, its desks the small coffins
> of lessons, its blackboards the tombstones of learning. The books
> in the Library stiffened and yellowed and curled. The portraits
> of gone Headmistresses stared into space. The school groaned,
> the tiles on its roof falling off in its sleep, its windows as white
> as chalk. The grass on the playing fields grew like grass
> on a grave.

Notice how Duffy uses imagery associated with death here. What is the effect of her calling the desks 'small coffins' or the blackboards 'tombstones'? Duffy develops an ordinary subversive act (the passing of a surreptitious note in the classroom) into a fantastic scenario involving the destruction of commonly accepted order and even the school building itself, which here serves as a symbol of all that may go wrong with institutionalised learning. The idea that formal education may be dull and deadening – just the opposite of what it ought to be – is neither new nor complicated (indeed, Duffy's language and some of her themes are clear, like Carolann's surname, 'Clare'), but look at how Duffy achieves more than this here. Duffy's simple and ordinary language prevents sentimentality, as does her characteristic use of humour, but there is nostalgia and sadness in these lines as well as satire.

▶ How does Duffy feel about the books in the library? The disintegration of the school building, with its windows 'white/as chalk'? How does Duffy feel about what happens to 'the playing fields'?

By the end of this 19-page poem, Carolann's note, which began as an attempt to embarrass the teacher's pet, has had a more powerful and wider effect than she could have intended or perhaps even imagined. The girls have inadvertently caused not only the closure of the school, but also the headmistress's subsequent breakdown – a fantasy probably familiar to many students. Even more dramatic and significant, however, is the ironic effect of the note: it liberates not the students so much as their teachers, most of whom Duffy describes in the final stanzas of the poem as fulfilling their suppressed dreams.

As Duffy focuses on the lives of the adult women, she enlarges the subject of her poem and extends its themes. Miss Dunn, the sports teacher, sets out to climb Mount Everest; the English teacher, Miss Nadimbaba, becomes a poet. The literature and geography teacher, who had required her class to memorise passages from Shakespeare and endless lists of the nation's rivers and lakes, leaves her dull husband and sets out to walk across Britain. Duffy writes that 'Mrs Mackay walked through Glen Strathfarrar, mad, muttering,/ free; a filthy old pack on her back filled with scavenged loot –/ banana, bottle, blanket, balaclava, bread, blade, bible.' Like Edna Pontellier in Kate Chopin's novel *The Awakening*, Mrs Mackay has neither the inner resources nor the social support to cope with her liberation:

> By dawn, at John O'Groats, Mrs Mackay had finally run out of land.
> She wrote her maiden name with a stick in the sand then walked
> into the sea, steady at first, step by step, till the firm waves lifted her
> under her arms and danced her away like a groom with a bride.

Miss Batt, the music and history teacher, and Miss Fife, head of maths, finally declare their love for one another and move 'to a city. They drank in a dark bar where women danced, cheek/ to cheek. Miss Batt loved Miss Fife till she sobbed and shook/ in her arms.'

This humorous, tender and bittersweet poem is finally passionate and, despite its direct language and apparent clarity, rich in allusion and serious themes. Miss Fife loves Miss Batt with a love that goes beyond desire for a particular individual. Duffy writes that Miss Fife dreams of the school as a sinking ship steered by a ghost whose face resembles each of the teachers in turn, suggesting her sisterhood with all of the female faculty. Her distress at the various fates of the other women in the poem is assuaged, however, when she wakes up beside Miss Batt, finding 'in the darkness, a face over hers, a warm mouth/ kissing the gibberish from her lips. The school sank in her mind,/ a black wave taking it down as she gazed at the woman's face.' When Mrs Mackay drowns, having written her name only in the sand, 'High above in the cold sky' seagulls laugh 'like schoolgirls' in a cosmic mockery that recalls Shakespeare's portrayal of the unfeeling gods in *King Lear* as well as the similar circling gulls at the end of Chopin's *The Awakening*. Yet 'The Laughter at Stafford Girls' High' does not end with death in an indifferent universe but with an affirmative renewal and rebirth. Duffy writes that 'Higher again, a teacher fell through the clouds with a girl in her arms.'

Duffy's readers

Who reads Carol Ann Duffy's work? *Mean Time*, a collection of poems published in 1993, has been taught as a set text for English A Levels, while her poems frequently appear in anthologies used in secondary schools. She is a popular reader of her own work and has been welcomed by young people with the sort of applause and cheers that would not be out of place at a rock concert. As 'The Laughter at Stafford Girls' High' suggests, however, Duffy's writing is by no means limited to any particular group of readers. While obviously feminist, she does not confine her work to 'female' subjects or issues in any narrow way, and she has received acclaim from the general public as well as from readers who have identified themselves as feminist, lesbian and gay. One of her poems in *Mean Time*, 'Café Royal', depicts a young man in London who wishes he could have saved Oscar Wilde from his trial for sodomy, subsequent conviction, imprisonment and lonely death in Paris. But this poem is not only about a dashing literary figure particularly admired by gay male readers; it is also about memory and how we make sense of history. Duffy has used her verse to address topical issues such as AIDS, yet however contemporary her poetry may seem – her informal, relaxed language often makes her work seem conversational and easily accessible – she invariably addresses larger issues concerning identity and the past, human passion and possibility.

Despite her popularity and the literary merits of her verse, Duffy's personal life and her willingness to speak out, as well as the fact that she is a woman were probably determining factors in her being denied the position of poet laureate after Ted Hughes' death in 1999. Duffy has called herself a lesbian poet, and lives with her female partner, the Scottish poet Jackie Kay (b. 1961), Kay's son and her own daughter. The British prime minister was reported to have been 'worried about having a homosexual as a poet laureate because of how it might play in middle England' (*The Sunday Times*, 9 May 1999). What do you suppose he meant by this? In the end, the decision was taken to offer the post to the accomplished poet and biographer Andrew Motion, who, as the journalist John Morrish pointed out, 'could hardly be more white, Oxbridge, English or male' (*The Independent on Sunday*, 18 April 1999). Duffy would have been the first woman laureate.

The challenge of Shakespeare's sister

Virginia Woolf concluded *A Room of One's Own* by returning to the subject of Shakespeare's sister, the woman writer who failed to realise her potential by virtue of being female. 'Living the life of Aphra Behn', as the fictional Judith Shakespeare tried to do, has always had consequences, as Duffy's recent failure to become poet laureate suggests. In the final chapter of her book, Woolf insisted that 'Intellectual freedom depends on material things. Poetry depends on intellectual freedom. And women have always been poor ... from the beginning of time.' Do you feel modern women writers still suffer from the dangers and 'poverty' Woolf is referring to here? In what ways?

Woolf finally turned her attention in *A Room of One's Own* to her audience – the female students at Cambridge University who first heard her book delivered as a series of lectures in 1928, but also her contemporary readers in 1929 and her future readers, us. Using an increasingly personal and emotional voice, she urged them 'to write all kinds of books, hesitating at no subject however trivial or however vast'. What evidence do you have that women writers have – or have not – hesitated to write what they really felt?

▶ Look at Carol Ann Duffy's poem 'White Writing' (Part 3, page 110). What does the speaker mean by 'white writing'? Consider all the things she lists that have not been written: vows, prayers, laws, rules, news, poems. What evidence does Duffy offer here to help us understand why these things have not been written? How does the speaker 'write them white' in this poem?

Recalling Judith Shakespeare, Woolf finally exhorted her audience to continue what she saw as a tradition of women's writing:

> Now my belief is that this poet who never wrote a word and was buried at the crossroads still lives. She lives in you and in me, and in many other

women who are not here tonight, for they are washing up the dishes and putting the children to bed. But she lives; for great poets do not die; they are continuing presences; they need only the opportunity to walk among us in the flesh. This opportunity, as I think, it is now coming within your power to give her. For my belief is that if we live another century ... and have five hundred a year each of us and rooms of our own; if we have the habit of freedom and the courage to write exactly what we think... then the opportunity will come and the dead poet who was Shakespeare's sister will put on the body which she has so often laid down.

What does Woolf mean when she insists that the fictional Judith Shakespeare 'still lives'? How can gifted writers be 'continuing presences' even if they have never written a word?

In the last paragraph of her essay, Woolf insisted that women would someday write the literature they were called to create. She urged her audience to help Judith Shakespeare to 'put on the body' she had so often sacrificed by continuing to read and to write no matter what obstacles might present themselves. Woolf's confidence in the future has been an inspiration, suggesting not only the especially challenging situations the woman writer has always faced, but the hope and conviction that, by understanding women writers in context, readers, too, can change the literary landscape. *A Room of One's Own* concludes with the author's reflections on Judith Shakespeare – not only the fictional sister who killed herself long ago, but the potential woman writer of the future. Here are Woolf's final words:

Drawing her life from the lives of the unknown who were her forerunners, as her brother did before her, she will be born. As for her coming without that preparation, without that effort on our part, without that determination that when she is born again she shall find it possible to live and write her poetry, that we cannot expect, for that would be impossible. But I maintain that she would come if we worked for her, and that so to work, even in poverty and obscurity, is worth while.

Assignments

1   In her essays and in her poetry, Adrienne Rich cites various methods that society and culture have historically used to discourage women's creativity. Look at the passages from two of her essays on page 105 of Part 3. According to Rich, in what ways does 'the power of men' work against women's writing? In what ways are Rich's points illustrated by Virginia Woolf's story of Shakespeare's sister, in Part 3, pages 94–95? In what ways are Rich's points illustrated in women's writing you have read or in women's lives that you know about?

2   Compare 'Mary Hamilton' with Virginia Woolf's account of Judith Shakespeare (Part 3, pages 81–83 and pages 94–95). How are they similar? In what ways do Mary Hamilton's and Judith Shakespeare's fates depend on particular historical circumstances of time and place? Can either or both of these stories be understood as containing universal truths about women's experience? Why or why not? How is your understanding of Woolf's account of Shakespeare's sister enriched by your awareness of the ballad written over three centuries earlier?

3   Consider Adrienne Rich's statements (Part 3, page 105) or the poem and passages from Margaret Atwood's work (Part 3, pages 105–108). What issues do Rich and Atwood address that Dickinson also raises in her poetry?

4   Look at Carol Ann Duffy's poem 'Anon' in Part 3, page 109. What is she saying here about the tradition of women writing that Woolf describes? What do you make of her use of the nonsense phrase 'hey nonny nonny', a refrain that frequently occurs in Renaissance lyrics and that Shakespeare sometimes uses in songs incorporated in his plays? Can you explain Duffy's title? Reflecting on what you have learned about women's writing, how does Duffy place 'Anon' within a continuing tradition? In what ways does an understanding of this female literary tradition enrich your understanding of this poem?

5   Look at the passage from Jane Austen's *Pride and Prejudice* in Part 3, pages 86–87. How does Austen use humour to convey her ideas about the importance of marriage and money to a woman in her society? Contrast Austen's views of what is important for a woman with those expressed by Lady Mary Wortley Montagu (Part 3, pages 84–85). You might also contrast Austen's ideas with those expressed by Charlotte Brontë in *Jane Eyre* (look particularly at Chapter XII). What accounts for the differences you find? What different – or similar – assumptions do these female authors make about human nature?

2 | Approaching the texts

- What kinds of texts do female authors write?

- What are the contexts for reading women's writing?

- How do women writers place their own work in context?

- What contexts have critics and other readers used?

Placing women writers in context

Women writers offer the reader a huge range of material. As in the case of male writers, the reader will need to look carefully at the woman writer's use of language, at the voice in the work, its tone and point of view. The reader will want to think as well about the subject of the work, its characters, setting, plot, and themes. Because women have also written in different cultures and languages from the beginning of history, the various contexts for reading their work are especially rich. Readers will need to begin by asking, 'What information is necessary to understand this writer's values and attitudes?' The reader will then want to ask more specifically, 'What did her society expect of her? How does her work respond to these expectations?' In answering such questions, the reader may also find it helpful to find out about the woman writer's life – unless, of course, she was anonymous – as well as the geographical place and the historical period in which she wrote.

Because so many women had difficulty getting their work published or chose for a variety of reasons to write texts (such as letters, journals or personal poems) which were circulated privately if at all, the reader will also need to consider the woman writer's audience. The reader will need to ask, 'Who read this text? Whom was it written for? What was its initial audience?' The reader may also want to know, 'What happened to this text after it was written? When was it published? Who has read it since?' Finally, the reader will surely want to ask, 'Who is reading this text now? What does it mean to read the work of this woman writer today?'

Another way of reading 'in context' is to read women's writing as in part a response to the literary conventions or movements of the author's era. For instance, we might read Jane Austen's work in the context of her contemporary Sir Walter Scott (1771–1832), a novelist she very much admired. We might read H.D.'s writing in the context of works by the other experimental writers who were also part of the 20th-century literary movement called Modernism (among them D.H. Lawrence, T.S. Eliot, James Joyce, and Virginia Woolf).

Work by women writers may also be read in the context of the important social and intellectual ideas of their times. For instance, H.D. was in the early 1930s a patient of the ground-breaking psychoanalyst Sigmund Freud (1856–1939). We might consider her writing in the context of Freud's essay 'Femininity' (an excerpt appears in Part 3, pages 95–97). Indeed, many people in the 20th century came to believe Freud's theories about female psychology. Looking at Sylvia Plath's writing, we can see her anguish as she tried to be the sort of woman Freud prescribed and as she rejected his ideas towards the end of her life. In a more contemporary context, we can read the American poet Emily Grosholz's 'Ithaka' (2002) in Part 3, page 108, as a feminist poem. We might also, however, want to understand this poem in the larger literary context in which it is set: Grosholz portrays Penelope, the faithful wife of Odysseus in Homer's epic, as a 'writer' who weaves her story into the tapestry that she also unweaves every night. Indeed, 'Ithaka' needs to be considered both as a response to Homer (and thus to the literary tradition that includes writing by men) and as a poem that the author presents as part of the long tradition of women's writing.

Any good piece of writing should certainly be able to stand on its own. A first reading often involves considering the work 'out of context': we may know little about the author, for example, or when or where she wrote; we may not even know the author's gender. Even so, we quickly come to the issue of context when, for instance, we find an unfamiliar word or a reference to an historical event or conventions with which we are unfamiliar. Then we need to do some homework. Reading in context may be especially important for understanding the work of women writers because of the particular challenges the woman writer has always faced and continues to face even today. A few specific contexts for reading women writers are discussed in greater detail on the following pages.

Biography

A woman's own life experiences can offer us an important context for reading her work. But what sources can we use to help us understand the life of a woman writer? Are some sources better than others? How can we use biography to help put a female author in context?

In *Writing a Woman's Life* (1997), the literary critic Carolyn Heilbrun indicates that there are many ways of 'writing a woman's life'. Biographers – both those contemporary with their subjects (like Elizabeth Gaskell, who wrote about Charlotte Brontë as a friend, a fellow writer and a gifted woman of her own time) and those who came after – have various agendas and interests when they construct the 'story' of a woman's life. What, for instance, are the prejudices that Frederic Rowton reveals in his short 'life' of Felicia Hemans (Part 3, page 88)? What values of his time does his 'biography' demonstrate?

It may seem relatively easy to notice Rowton's preconceptions because most of us no longer share them; it can be much more difficult to see the 'agenda' in modern criticism. Consider the impression we get of H.D. from the feminist critics Sandra Gilbert and Susan Gubar in *The Norton Anthology of Literature by Women* (1985). They point out that:

> If, as the literary critic Rachel Blau DuPlessis has shown, H.D. sometimes seemed inextricably drawn to a relationship of 'romantic thralldom' with such men [as Richard Aldington, the American poet Ezra Pound and D.H. Lawrence], what she took away from them was transformed into a revisionary mythology that reflected her lifelong effort to understand her identity as a woman and a poet.

Gilbert and Gubar portray H.D. as 'The only surviving daughter in a prominent family that included five sons', and indicate that she received a good education, attending Bryn Mawr College, a prestigious university, which she soon left, 'after failing English and suffering from a breakdown'. They write that H.D. 'analysed the conflict she experienced at this time between her relationship with the young Ezra Pound, to whom she became engaged, and her growing attachment to a girlfriend, Frances Gregg'. Gilbert and Gubar also describe how, in 1919, H.D. was 'saved' – from a crisis brought about by the horrors of the First World War, her failing marriage, pregnancy with a child who was not her husband's, and pneumonia – 'by the intercession of the 24-year-old woman who would befriend her for the rest of her life, the writer Winifred Ellerman – or Bryher, as she called herself (after one of the Scilly Islands)'. Gubar and Gilbert go on to note that on a visit to Greece with Bryher in 1920 'H.D. had one of her first psychic or visionary experiences ... The two women felt they had glimpsed a narrative line that, moving beyond the destruction of modern culture to a vision of female regeneration, would inform H.D.'s later poetry.'

▶ What particular interests do Gubar and Gilbert reveal here? Look carefully at all the words in this 'biography' that portray H.D. as a female hero. Stressing H.D.'s salvation by her lesbian friend Bryher, Gilbert and Gubar emphasise female solidarity, but they do not mention the word 'lesbian' when describing H.D.'s relationship with either Bryher or Frances Gregg. What does their description gain from this omission? Do you think it loses anything? Now compare this portrait of H.D. and Rowton's depiction of Hemans: what cultural differences might account for the differences you find?

Gilbert and Gubar, both modern feminists, as well as Rowton, a man of Victorian sensibilities, reflect their own time and place in their 'biographies'; indeed, they tell us as much about the various contexts which influence particular readers as about the women writers and their writing.

Autobiography

In their description of H.D., Gilbert and Gubar are careful to draw on her own autobiographical writings, using them as authoritative documents. Indeed, Heilbrun indicates that some women write their own lives by writing autobiographies. Women also write their own lives in other literary genres, such as diaries or letters or autobiographical fiction, of which H.D.'s *Bid Me to Live* or Sylvia Plath's *The Bell Jar* are good examples. Specifically, when Gilbert and Gubar use the word 'saved' to describe Bryher's helpfulness to H.D. in 1919, they are quoting H.D., who uses this word in a similar situation in *Paint It Today* (1992), an autobiographical novel published posthumously, but written in the mid-1920s, after she had left Aldington and was living near Bryher in Switzerland. Should you trust H.D. in her version of her own life? Why or why not? What factors might influence the way a woman writes her own life? What impact should these factors have on our understanding of a woman writer's life and work? Autobiography like biography needs to be read in context. Such a reading, although challenging, can provide a richer understanding of both the writer and her work.

Heilbrun goes even further, however, to suggest that women write their own lives by living them. That is, women 'script' their lives, whether they follow the cultural scripts offered to them – which they may internalise and affirm, or may follow only reluctantly – or whether they rebel against social norms or expectations and live in ways beyond their culture's prescriptions. For women writers, who by the very act of writing have invariably done something not every woman or person does, this scripting of their own lives has brought with it difficult challenges.

▶ Look at Ban Zhao's 'Admonitions for Girls' (Part 3, page 80). What 'admonitions' here would have made writing difficult, if not impossible, for a young woman in early China?

It may be much easier to be a woman writer now than even a hundred years ago, but depending on her culture, a woman writer today continues to face often insuperable difficulties. She continues to be defined and often disenfranchised by, for instance, her colour, her class, her sexual orientation or her religious background. What is it like to be a woman writer today in Iran, in India, in Africa or in rural South America? What is it like to be a woman writer in a country wracked by war, as recently in Chechnya or Iraq? What are the different conditions that influence a woman writing now in, for example, Israel or Northern Ireland or New York City? How free are such women writers to script their own lives? You might even consider if a woman needs to be 'free' in order to write. Might some writing indeed be enriched by the very constrictions that also constrain it?

Women and madness

'Madness' has often been used to dismiss or trivialise women writers. When Sandra Gilbert and Susan Gubar wrote their first book together on women writers, they called it *The Madwoman in the Attic* (1979). Their title suggests one challenge faced by many women writers: for a woman to write is to be out-of-the-ordinary, perhaps to be mad or at least to be perceived as mad. In her short story 'The Yellow Wallpaper' (1892), Charlotte Perkins Gilman examines the madness that follows the restrictions placed on the female protagonist as, forbidden to put pen to paper, she becomes increasingly dissatisfied with the patriarchal forces that constrain and oppress her in her society. In *Jane Eyre*, Charlotte Brontë depicts Bertha Rochester as the mad wife whom Jane will replace. The author indirectly asks us to consider if to marry a man like Rochester is perhaps to be mad or to be driven mad.

Not to marry is also to court a kind of madness – or to be perceived by others as mad. Before feminist critics began to re-read Dickinson in the 1970s, she was often portrayed by scholars as a peculiar woman, a woman with whom something must have gone wrong. Such traditional readers frequently wondered why she never married, and many studies of Dickinson and her poetry spent a great deal of time looking for possible suitors or traumas in her life rather than looking at the conditions in her life that made her writing possible.

▶ Consider what Emily Dickinson herself has to say on the subject of the female writer and madness in poem 435 (Part 3, page 90). To whom does the 'discerning Eye' belong? What is gained by her use of the feminine word 'Demur' rather than, for example, a word such as 'protest'?

Literary critics have sometimes treated Virginia Woolf in a similar way. Woolf experienced her first breakdown at the age of 13 and endured subsequent periods of severe depression and psychosis throughout her life before committing suicide by drowning in 1941. She is still sometimes presented as a woman who wrote despite her madness. As in the case of a gifted writer like Sylvia Plath, we need to ask rather to what degree going against cultural expectations – whether or not such rebellion results in 'madness' or even suicide – shapes the writing that results, to what degree 'madness' is an enabling factor without which the writing might not have been possible.

Today we also need to guard against the opposite impulse: to discount the merits of women writers who do not seem rebellious or even feminist.

▶ Phyllis McGinley's 'The 5:32' (Part 3, pages 97–98) offers a good example of a poem that some readers might be tempted to dismiss because the speaker seems fulfilled by her traditional role. What elements in this poem might suggest complacency? Could you defend this poem as both accomplished and emotionally honest?

Genre

Because women writers have often chosen to express themselves in genres we may not be used to reading as literature, we may want to consider the conventions of a particular genre as a context for their work. How does Margaret Atwood draw on the conventions of the newspaper report in 'Questions Raised in City Death' (Part 3, page 107), the fictional report that forms part of the first chapter of *The Blind Assassin* (2000)? Laura Chase and her sister Iris ('Mrs. Richard E. Griffen') are the central characters in this historical novel that also draws on the conventions of the detective story and the mystery novel. How does Atwood use this 'report' to suggest the dynamics of the narrative that will follow?

In contrast, what are the conventions of journals or diaries? In these genres an author can perhaps express her innermost thoughts and feelings precisely because there is no 'real' audience. A good example is *Anne Frank: The Diary of a Young Girl* (1952). In this text, written while in hiding from Nazi persecution, the young Jewish writer Anne Frank (1929–1945) invents a friend, an alter-ego called 'Kitty', to whom she addresses her 'letters'. Frank writes in her first entry, 'I hope I shall be able to confide in you completely, as I have never been able to do in anyone before, and I hope that you will be a great support and comfort to me.' (translated B.M. Mooyaart-Doubleday, 1952)

This tradition of private, potentially intimate writing has sometimes resulted in 'confessional writing', such as Plath's *The Bell Jar*, in which the author uses a personal, autobiographical voice to express what may not usually be voiced in public.

▶ Consider, for example, the American novelist Erica Jong's *Fanny* (1980), an excerpt from which appears in Part 3, pages 103–104. Jong's narrator is Fanny Hackabout Jones, a young woman in 18th-century England who wants to be a writer and indeed 'writes' the novel as a long 'confessional' letter to her daughter, Belinda. What 'confessional' elements do you find here? How does Jong (or Fanny) use the confession both to justify her choice of subject (a rape) and to reveal the oppressive attitudes towards women in her society?

Contexts suggested by the author

Authors often suggest, directly or indirectly, other contexts for reading their work, for example, through a dedication, as in Erica Jong's 'Alcestis on the Poetry Circuit' (1973; Part 3, pages 101–103); through an allusion, as in Jong's poem and in Carol

Ann Duffy's 'Anon' (Part 3, page 109); or through a setting, as in Plath's 'Wuthering Heights' (Part 3, pages 99–100), in which she recounts a visit to the place referred to in Emily Brontë's novel.

A further common context for a literary text is another literary text. For instance, Emily Grosholz uses the ancient Greek story of Penelope and her suitors for the reflections in 'Ithaka' (Part 3, page 108). Sometimes a literary work can even be a rewriting of another literary work, as in Jean Rhys's *Wide Sargasso Sea* (1966), in which she offers a 'rereading' of *Jane Eyre* by focusing on what happened in Jamaica when the young Rochester courted Bertha (whom Rhys calls Antoinette). Similarly, in *Fanny*, Jong 're-writes' the 18th-century pornographer John Cleland's *Fanny Hill*. In such works, the author invites the reader to learn about other literary texts as a way of enriching their work while simultaneously placing their own work within the context of a larger literary tradition. As Adrienne Rich suggests in her volume of essays *On Lies, Secrets, and Silence* (excerpts appear in Part 3, page 105), such contextualising may be particularly significant for women writers, who have often been denied a literary tradition.

Literary criticism

We can also think of literary criticism – either by women writers themselves, by their contemporaries, by earlier or later writers, or by scholars – as yet another context for understanding women's writing. In *Advertisements for Myself* (1966) the American critic Norman Mailer made what he called a 'terrible confession': 'I have nothing to say about any of the talented women who write today … I do not seem able to read them.'

▶ How do you respond to such a statement? What is Mailer saying about women writers and their work in 1966? What is he saying about himself? What does his 'terrible confession' tell us about how to read? Do you think his statement is serious or is he joking? What does his attitude towards women writers teach you about reading?

The contemporary critic Annette Kolodny has argued that 'all readers, male and female alike, must be taught first to recognise the existence of a significant body of writing by women … and, second, they must be encouraged to learn how to read it within its own unique and informing contexts …' (from 'A Map for Rereading: Gender and the Interpretation of Literary Texts' [1980]. *The New Feminist Criticism*, ed. Elaine Showalter 1986).

Our own context

As Mailer's remarks suggest, another context which we inevitably bring to our reading, though we may not be entirely conscious of it, is the context of our own lives and times. Given the contemporary emphasis in most modern societies on the formal education of girls as well as boys, we may not today find Lady Mary Wortley Montagu's advice to her daughter so very radical as it was in her own time. In today's relatively permissive atmosphere, we may not be shocked by Mary Wollstonecraft's ideas about women's suffrage or even by Erica Jong's irreverence and frankness in her depiction of Alexander Pope (Part 3, pages 103–104).

Our own reading today has also been influenced by modern feminism, whether or not we choose to call ourselves feminists.

▶ Look at Plath's 'Ode for Ted' in Part 3, pages 98–99. How do you suppose readers reacted to this poem when it appeared in Plath's first collection of verse, *The Colossus*, in 1960? Do we read this poem now with a greater sense of irony and scepticism than Ted Hughes or Plath's mother, early readers of this poem soon after it was written in 1956? What do you feel accounts for these differences in understanding?

While not falling into the trap Mailer reveals in his 'terrible confession', we should also be aware that we care about and respond especially deeply to literature which speaks to our own experiences and feelings. If women writers – like all writers – write out of their own context, their own lives and cultures, can male readers or any readers in a different time and place understand them? What special efforts may be necessary for the male reader, for example, approaching a text by a female author? We may also want to think about how we read male writers; we need to think about whether and in what ways all readers, male and female, may have been taught to read literature from a particular perspective.

▶ Read Jong's 'Alcestis on the Poetry Circuit' (Part 3, pages 101–103). What does the author suggest here about how women perceive themselves? What does she suggest about how readers perceive women writers?

The writer's work as a context

Perhaps the most important context for a particular text by a particular writer, however, is the rest of that writer's work. Thus the extracts included in Part 3 are best understood within the context of the works from which they are taken, although in this book they are offered primarily as contexts for other works. Women writers in this volume are sometimes represented by several poems or extracts because these other texts provide a context, a sort of commentary on the rest of their work.

Look, for instance, at the poems by Emily Dickinson in Part 3, pages 88–91. How would you characterise the voice of the speaker in poem 101? If this were the only evidence of the author's attitude towards God and religious faith, you might conclude that Dickinson was a childish believer, coy and even simple in her spiritual understanding. But Dickinson is a skilful poet of many different moods and brilliantly understands not only the desire for faith but the frustrations and anger of religious doubt. Reading a few poems by one author on a similar subject can give you a broader understanding of her complexity and deepen your appreciation of her achievement.

Early, middle and late work may illustrate interesting changes as well as continuities over the course of a woman writer's career. Work written at about the same time may show, through repetition, the depth of her convictions or – as in the case of Emily Dickinson – different or conflicting moods or attitudes. Rather than relying on someone else's selection, you might read independently an entire collection of poems, two or three stories or novels by one female author. The most appropriate or interesting contexts are likely to be those you choose and research yourself.

Assignments

1 Read the poems by Emily Dickinson in Part 3, pages 88–91. How would you characterise the speakers in poems 338 and 243? What is Dickinson saying about faith when she compares it to a circus tent? When she writes 'I know that He exists', does she reveal her confirmed belief or her bitter doubt? How is poem 101 enriched by being read within the context of these two other poems? How are poems 338 and 243 complicated by your understanding of the naive but sincere and willing searching by the speaker in poem 101?

2 Throughout her life Dickinson returned repeatedly to topics and problems of particular interest to her. Look at poems 288, 303, 308 and 441 in Part 3, pages 89–91. What do these poems, read in the context of each other, tell you about Dickinson's view of poetry and the creative process? What does poem 308 tell you about sunsets? Is this poem not only about sunsets but also about nature and female expression? What do poems 199 and 435 (Part 1, page 52, and Part 3, page 90) tell you about female psychology?

3 Look at the two texts by Erica Jong in Part 3, pages 101–104. In what ways does the young Fanny behave like 'the best slave' in 'Alcestis on the Poetry Circuit'? While Jong's poem is explicitly about her feminist beliefs, in what ways are these beliefs developed further in her novel? What is gained by Jong's use of an 18th-century historical context? What is gained (or lost) by her changing genre, by her shifting from verse to fiction?

4   Look at what Adrienne Rich has to say about the social forces that work against women's creative expression in the excerpts from her essays in Part 3, page 105. In what ways does Poem XIII from 'Twenty–One Love Poems' (Part 3, page 104) address the same issues? In what ways is this a political poem? In what ways is this a love poem? On the basis of what you know of Rich's work, do you think for her the two subjects – love and politics – are different? Is there a difference between the two for you?

5   Compare Margaret Atwood's 'Spelling' and Carol Ann Duffy's 'White Writing' (Part 3, pages 105–106 and page 110). Both women focus on the challenges that face the woman writer. What are the differences between them? You might consider specifically each poem's tone, subject, situation, and images. To what degree can you attribute some of the differences between these two poems to the different eras in which they were published, 1981 and 2002? Atwood's poem is contemporary with, for instance, the excerpts from Adrienne Rich in Part 3, page 104, while Duffy's poem is more recent. How does what you know about Duffy's life (see Part 1, page 64, and pages 66–67) help you to understand the context of 'White Writing'?

6   Read carefully the passage from Sigmund Freud's work that appears in Part 3, pages 95–97. How might Freud have used the ideas he expresses here to analyse Judith Shakespeare, as depicted by Virginia Woolf in the passage in Part 3, pages 94–95? How might he have responded to the speaker of Stevie Smith's 'Papa Love Baby' (Part 3, page 97)? How might you argue against a Freudian interpretation of women's experience as presented by these female authors?

3 | Texts and extracts

The texts and extracts that follow have been chosen to illustrate key themes and points made elsewhere in the book, and to provide material which may be useful when working on the assignments. The items are arranged chronologically.

Ban Zhao

From 'Admonitions for Girls' (c. 100)

Humility means yielding and acting respectful, putting others first and oneself last, never mentioning one's own good deeds or denying one's own faults, enduring insults and bearing with mistreatment, all with due trepidation. Industriousness means going to bed late, getting up early, never shirking work morning or night, never refusing to take on domestic work, and completing everything that needs to be done neatly and carefully. Continuing the sacrifices means serving one's husband-master with appropriate demeanour, keeping oneself clean and pure, never joking or laughing, and preparing pure wine and food to offer the ancestors. There has never been a woman who had these three traits and yet ruined her reputation or fell into disgrace. On the other hand, if a woman lacks these three traits, she will have no name to preserve and will not be able to avoid shame.

Li Ch'ing-chao

Two translations of the poem 'A Twig of Mume Blossoms' (c. 1120); the first translation is by Xu Yuan Zhong (1994); the second translation is by Liu Wu-chi (1966)

A Twig of Mume Blossoms
Pink fragrant lotus fade; autumn chills mat of jade.
My silk robe doffed, I float
Alone in orchid boat.
Who in the cloud would bring me letters in brocade?
When swans come back in flight,
My bower's steeped in moonlight.

As fallen flowers drift and water runs their way,
One longing overflows
Two places with same woes.
Such sorrow can by no means be driven away;
From eyebrows kept apart,
Again it gnaws my heart.

A Sprig of Plum Blossoms

Fragrance fades away from the red lotus-roots;
The lovely bamboo mat becomes cold in autumn.
Gently loosening his silk robe,
He mounts alone the magnolia boat.
Who would have sent an embroidered letter from among the clouds?
When the message comes back from the wild goose,
The moon has filled the western chamber.

Flowers fall and waters flow by themselves.
It is the same kind of yearning –
An idle sorrow in two different places.
This sadness cannot be dispersed or banished:
It has just left the eyebrows
When once again it enters the heart.

Anonymous

From 'Mary Hamilton' (16th century)

Mary Hamilton

Word's gane to the kitchen
   And word's gane to the ha,
That Marie Hamilton gangs wi bairn
   To the hichest Stewart of a'.

He's courted her in the kitchen,
   He's courted her in the ha,
He's courted her in the laigh cellar,
   And that was warst of a'.

She's tyed it in her apron
   And she's thrown it in the sea;
Says, 'Sink ye, swim ye, bonny wee babe!
   You'l neer get mair o me.'

Down then cam the auld queen,
   Goud tassels tying her hair:
'O Marie, where's the bonny wee babe
   That I heard greet sae sair?'

'There never was a babe intill my room,
    As little designs to be;
It was but a touch o my sair side,
    Came over my fair bodie.'

'O Marie, put on your robes o black,
    Or else your robes o brown,
For ye maun gang wi me the night,
    To see fair Edinbro town.'

'I winna put on my robes o black,
    Nor yet my robes o brown;
But I'll put on my robes o white,
    To shine through Edinbro town.'

When she gaed up the Cannogate,
    She laughd loud laughters three;
But whan she cam down the Cannogate
    The tear blinded her ee.

When she gaed up the Parliament stair,
    The heel cam aff her shee;
And lang or she cam down again
    She was condemned to dee.

When she cam down the Cannogate,
    The Cannogate sae free,
Many a ladie lookd oer her window,
    Weeping for this ladie.

'Ye need nae weep for me,' she says,
    'Ye need nae weep for me;
For had I not slain mine own sweet babe,
    This death I wadna dee.

'Bring me a bottle of wine,' she says,
    'The best that eer ye hae,
That I may drink to my weil-wishers,
    And they may drink to me...'

'Here's a health to the jolly sailors,
    That sail upon the sea;
Let them never let on to my father and mother
    That I cam here to dee ...

WOMEN'S WRITING: PAST AND PRESENT

'Last night I washd the queen's feet'
    And gently laid her down;
And a' the thanks I've gotten the nicht
    To be hangd in Edinbro town!

'Last nicht there was four Maries
    The nicht there'l be but three;
There was Marie Seton, and Marie Beton,
    And Marie Carmichael, and me.'

Anne Bradstreet

'The Author to Her Book' (1678)

The Author to Her Book
Thou ill-form'd offspring of my feeble brain,
Who after birth did'st by my side remain,
Till snatcht from thence by friends, less wise then true,
Who thee abroad, expos'd to publick view,
Made thee in raggs, halting to th'press to trudge,
Where errors were not lessened (all may judge).
At thy return my blushing was not small,
My rambling brat (in print) should mother call,
I cast thee by as one unfit for light,
Thy Visage was so irksome in my sight;
Yet being mine own, at length affection would
Thy blemishes amend, if so I could:
I wash'd thy face, but more defects I saw,
And rubbing off a spot, still made a flaw.
I stretcht thy joynts to make thee even feet,
Yet still thou run'st more hobling then is meet;*
In better dress to trim thee was my mind,
But nought save home-spun Cloth i'th'house I find.
In this array, 'mongst Vulgars* mayst thou roam.
In Criticks hands, beware thou dost not come,
And take thy way where yet thou art not known
If for thy Father askt, say, thou hadst none:
And for thy Mother, she alas is poor,
Which caus'd her thus to send thee out of door.

---

meet appropriate   **vulgars** common people

Lady Mary Wortley Montagu

From 'To the Countess of Bute, Lady Montagu's Daughter' (28 January 1753)

Dear Child, – You have given me a great deal of satisfaction by your account of your eldest daughter. I am particularly pleased to hear she is a good arithmetician; it is the best proof of understanding: the knowledge of numbers is one of the chief distinctions between us and the brutes.* If there is anything in blood, you may reasonably expect your children should be endowed with an uncommon share of good sense ...

I will therefore speak to you as supposing [her] ... not only capable, but desirous of learning: in that case by all means let her be indulged in it ... Learning, if she has a real taste for it, will not only make her contented, but happy in it. No entertainment is so cheap as reading, nor any pleasure so lasting. She will not want new fashions, nor regret the loss of expensive diversions, or variety of company, if she can be amused with an author in her closet.* To render this amusement extensive, she should be permitted to learn the languages. I have heard it lamented that boys lose so many years in mere learning of words: this is no objection to a girl, whose time is not so precious: she cannot advance herself in any profession, and has therefore more hours to spare: and as you say her memory is good, she will be very agreeably employed this way.

There are two cautions to be given on this subject: first, not to think herself learned when she can read Latin, or even Greek. Languages are more properly to be called vehicles of learning than learning itself, as may be observed in many schoolmasters, who, though perhaps critics in grammar, are the most ignorant fellows upon earth. True knowledge consists in knowing things, not words. I would wish her no further a linguist than to enable her to read books in their originals that are often corrupted, and always injured by translations. Two hours' application every morning will bring this about much sooner than you can imagine and she will have leisure enough besides to run over the English poetry, which is a more important part of a woman's education than it is generally supposed ...

The second caution to be given her (and which is most absolutely necessary) is to conceal whatever learning she attains, with as much solicitude as she would hide crookedness or lameness; the parade of it can only serve to draw on her the envy, and consequently the most inveterate hatred, of all he and she fools, which will certainly be at least three parts in four of all her acquaintance. The use of knowledge in our sex, besides the amusement of solitude, is to moderate the passions, and learn to be contented with a small expense which are the certain effects of a studious life; and it may be

preferable even to that fame which men have engrossed to *
themselves, and will not suffer us to share. You will tell me I have not
observed this rule myself: but you are mistaken: it is only inevitable
accident that has given me any reputation that way. I have always
carefully avoided it and ever thought it a misfortune.

... If she has the same inclination (I should say passion) for
learning that I was born with [,] history, geography, and philosophy
will furnish her with materials to pass away cheerfully a longer life
than is allotted to mortals. I believe there are few heads capable of
making Sir I. Newton's calculations, but the result of them is not
difficult to be understood by a moderate capacity. Do not fear this
should make her affect the character of Lady — or Lady —, or Mrs. —
Those women are ridiculous, not because they have learning but
because they have it not. One thinks herself a complete historian
after reading Echard's Roman History; another a profound
philosopher, having got by heart some of Pope's unintelligible essays;
and a third an able divine,* on the strength of [the Methodist
preacher George] Whitefield's sermons: thus you hear them
screaming politics and controversy. It is a saying of [the Greek
historian] Thucydides, ignorance is bold, and knowledge reserved.
Indeed, it is impossible to be far advanced in it without being more
humbled by a conviction of human ignorance, than elated by learning.

---

brutes animals   **engrossed to** claimed for
closet bedroom   **divine** theologian

Anonymous

'Pretty Polly Oliver' (late 18th century)

Pretty Polly Oliver
As pretty Polly Oliver
Sat musing, 'tis said,
A comical fancy
Came into her head;
Nor father nor mother
Shall make me false prove,
I'll list for a soldier
And follow my love.

So in soldier's attire
To the wars she went out,
And bore a brave part
In both raid and in rout;
In the battle she found him
Slightly wounded and low
On the ground where he lay
With his face to the foe.

Now Polly he knew
In a moment's quick glance,
And he cried, Why my dear,
Sure I've met you in France;
But the lass she said, nay,
He was surely mistook,
But her words were belied
By the love in her look.

The sergeant sent for
The parson to come,
And couple the lovers
Who'd follow'd the drum;
And Polly, restored to
Her womanly state,
Found all she had sought
In a home and a mate.

Jane Austen

From *Pride and Prejudice* (1813)

It is a truth universally acknowledged, that a single man in possession of a good fortune, must be in want of a wife.

However little known the feelings or views of such a man may be on his first entering a neighbourhood, this truth is so well fixed in the minds of the surrounding families, that he is considered as the rightful property of some one or other of their daughters.

'My dear Mr. Bennet,' said his lady to him one day, 'have you heard that Netherfield Park is let at last?'

Mr. Bennet replied that he had not.

'But it is,' returned she; 'for Mrs. Long has just been here, and she told me all about it.'

Mr. Bennet made no answer.

'Do not you want to know who has taken it?' cried his wife impatiently.

'*You* want to tell me, and I have no objection to hearing it.'

This was invitation enough.

'Why, my dear, you must know, Mrs. Long says that Netherfield is taken by a young man of large fortune from the north of England; that he came down on Monday in a chaise and four to see the place, and was so much delighted with it that he agreed with Mr. Morris immediately; that he is to take possession before Michaelmas, and some of his servants are to be in the house by the end of next week.'

'What is his name?'

'Bingley.'

'Is he married or single?'

'Oh! single, my dear, to be sure! A single man of large fortune; four or five thousand a year. What a fine thing for our girls!'

Elizabeth Barrett Browning

'To George Sand' (1844)

To George Sand
  A Desire
Thou large-brained woman and large-hearted man,
Self-called George Sand! whose soul, amid the lions
Of thy tumultuous senses, moans defiance
And answers roar for roar, as spirits can:
I would some mild miraculous thunder ran
Above the applauded circus, in appliance
Of thine own nobler nature's strength and science,
Drawing two pinions,* white as wings of swan,
From thy strong shoulders, to amaze the place
With holier light! that thou to woman's claim
And man's, mightst join beside the angel's grace
Of a pure genius sanctified from blame,
Till child and maiden pressed to thine embrace
To kiss upon thy lips a stainless fame.

---

pinions wings

Frederic Rowton

From 'Felicia Hemans' (1853)

I think there can be no doubt that Mrs. Hemans takes decidedly one of the most prominent places among our Female Poets. She seems to me to represent and unite as purely and completely as any other writer in our literature the peculiar and specific qualities of the female mind. Her works are to my mind a perfect embodiment of a woman's soul: I would say that they are *intensely* feminine. The delicacy, the softness, the pureness, the quick observant vision, the ready sensibility, the devotedness, the faith of woman's nature find in Mrs. Hemans their ultra representative. The very diffuseness of her style is feminine, ... Diction, manner, sentiment, passion, and belief are in her as delicately *rounded off* as are the bones and muscles of the Medicean Venus. There is not a harsh or angular line in her whole mental contour. I do not know a violent, spasmodic, or contorted idea in all her writings; but every page is full of grace, harmony, and expressive glowing beauty.

In nothing can one trace her feminine spirit more strikingly than in her domestic home-loving ideas ... Mrs. Hemans has all the harmony of expression, all the subtle perfection and refined love of beauty, which distinguish her sex. Her verses are at once pictures and music ... But, after all, it is chiefly in the strength of her religious sentiment that Mrs. Hemans most completely typifies and represents her sex ...

Emily Dickinson

Poems 101, 249, 288, 303, 308, 320, 435, 441, 657 from *The Complete Poems of Emily Dickinson*, ed. Thomas H. Johnson (1955)

101
Will there really be a 'Morning'?
Is there such a thing as 'Day'?
Could I see it from the mountains
If I were as tall as they?

Has it feet like Water lilies?
Has it feathers like a Bird?
Is it brought from famous countries
Of which I have never heard?

Oh some Scholar! Oh some Sailor!
Oh some Wise Man from the skies!
Please to tell a little Pilgrim
Where the place called 'Morning' lies!

(1859)

249

Wild Nights – Wild Nights!
Were I with thee
Wild Nights should be
Our luxury!

Futile – the Winds –
To a Heart in port –
Done with the Compass –
Done with the Chart!

Rowing in Eden –
Ah, the Sea!
Might I but moor – Tonight –
In Thee!

(1861)

288

I'm Nobody! Who are you?
Are you – Nobody – Too?
Then there's a pair of us?
Don't tell! they'd advertise – you know!

How dreary – to be – Somebody!
How public– like a Frog –
To tell one's name – the livelong June –
To an admiring Bog!

(1861)

303

The Soul selects her own Society –
Then – shuts the Door –
To her divine Majority –
Present no more –

Unmoved – she notes the Chariots – pausing –
At her low Gate –
Unmoved – an Emperor be kneeling
Upon her Mat –

I've known her – from an ample nation –
Choose One –
Then – close the Valves of her attention –
Like Stone –

(1862)

308

I send Two Sunsets –
Day and I – in competition ran –
I finished Two – and several Stars –
While He – was making One –

His own was ampler – but as I
Was saying to a friend –
Mine – is the more convenient
To Carry in the Hand –

(1862)

320

We play at Paste –
Till qualified, for Pearl –
Then, drop the Paste –
And deem ourself a fool –

The Shapes – though – were similar –
And our new Hands
Learned *Gem*-Tactics –
Practicing *Sands* –

(1862)

435

Much Madness is divinest Sense –
To a discerning Eye –
Much Sense – the starkest Madness –
'Tis the Majority
In this, as All, prevail –
Assent – and you are sane –
Demur – you're straightway dangerous –
And handled with a Chain –

(1862)

WOMEN'S WRITING: PAST AND PRESENT

441
This is my letter to the World
That never wrote to Me –
The simple News that Nature told –
With tender Majesty

Her Message is committed
To Hands I cannot see –
For love of Her – Sweet – countrymen –
Judge tenderly – of Me

              (1862)

657
I dwell in Possibility –
A fairer House than Prose –
More numerous of Windows –
Superior – for Doors –

Of Chambers as the Cedars –
Impregnable of Eye –
And for an Everlasting Roof
The Gambrels of the Sky –

Of Visitors – the fairest –
For Occupation – This –
The spreading wide my narrow Hands
To gather Paradise –

              (1862)

Lydia Maria Child

'Diary Entry for 1864'

Wrote 235 letters.
Wrote 6 articles for newspapers.
Wrote 47 autograph articles for Fairs.
Wrote my Will.
Corrected Proofs for Sunset book.
Read aloud 6 pamphlets and 21 volumes.
Read to myself 7 volumes.

———

Made 25 needle books for Freedwomen.
2 Bivouac caps for soldiers.
Knit 2 pair of hospital socks.
Gathered and made peck of pickles for hospitals.
Knit 1 pair of socks for David.
Knit and made up 2 pairs of suspenders for D.
Knit six baby shirts for friends ...
Cut and made three gowns.
1 shirt with waist.
1 thick cotton petticoat.
1 quilted petticoat.
made 1 silk gown ...
Made a starred crib quilt, and quilted it, one fortnights work.

———

Spent 4 days collecting and sorting papers & pamphlets scattered by
   the fire.
Mended five pair of drawers.
Mended 70 pair of stockings.
Cooked 360 dinners.
Cooked 362 breakfasts.
Swept and dusted sitting-room & kitchen 350 times.
Filled lamps 362 times ...
Made 5 visits to aged women.
Tended upon invalid friend two days.
Made one day's visit to Medford and 3 visits to Boston ...
Made 7 calls upon neighbors.
Cut and dried half a peck of dried apples.

Kate Chopin

From *The Awakening* (1899)

She went on and on. She remembered the night she swam far out,
and recalled the terror that seized her at the fear of being unable to
regain the shore. She did not look back now, but went on and on,
thinking of the blue-grass meadow that she had traversed when a
little child, believing that it had no beginning and no end.

Her arms and legs were growing tired.

She thought of Léonce and the children. They were a part of her life.
But they need not have thought that they could possess her, body and
soul. How Mademoiselle Reisz would have laughed, perhaps sneered, if
she knew! 'And you call yourself an artist! What pretensions, Madame!

The artist must possess the courageous soul that dares and defies.'

Exhaustion was pressing upon and over-powering her.

... [Robert] did not know; he did not understand. He would never understand. Perhaps Doctor Mandelet would have understood if she had seen him – but it was too late; the shore was far behind her, and her strength was gone.

She looked into the distance, and the old terror flamed up for an instant, then sank again. Edna heard her father's voice and her sister Margaret's. She heard the barking of an old dog that was chained to the sycamore tree. The spurs of the cavalry officer clanged as he walked across the porch. There was the hum of bees, and the musky odor of pinks filled the air.

Virginia Woolf

From *A Room of One's Own* (1929)

[The Manx Cat]

If by good luck there had been an ash-tray handy, if one had not knocked the ash out of the window in default, if things had been a little different from what they were, one would not have seen, presumably, a cat without a tail. The sight of that abrupt and truncated animal padding softly across the quadrangle changed by some fluke of the subconscious intelligence the emotional light for me. It was as if someone had let fall a shade. Perhaps the excellent hock was relinquishing its hold. Certainly, as I watched the Manx cat pause in the middle of the lawn as if it too questioned the universe, something seemed lacking, something seemed different. But what was lacking, what was different, I asked myself ...

... A book lay beside me and, opening it, I turned casually enough to Tennyson ...

> She is coming, my dove, my dear;
>> She is coming, my life, my fate ...

Was that what men hummed at luncheon parties before the war? And the women?

> My heart is like a singing bird ...
> My heart is like an apple tree ...
> My heart is like a rainbow shell ...
> My heart is gladder than all these
>> Because my love is come to me.

Was that what women hummed at luncheon parties before the war?

There was something so ludicrous in thinking of people humming such things even under their breath at luncheon parties before the war that I burst out laughing, and had to explain my laughter by pointing at the Manx cat, who did look a little absurd, poor beast, without a tail, in the middle of the lawn. Was he really born so, or had he lost his tail in an accident? The tailless cat, though some are said to exist in the Isle of Man, is rarer than one thinks. It is a queer animal, quaint rather than beautiful. It is strange what a difference a tail makes – you know the sort of things one says as a lunch party breaks up and people are finding their coats and hats.

[The Spider's Web]
What were the conditions in which women lived, I asked myself; for fiction, imaginative work, that is, is not dropped like a pebble upon the ground, as science may be; fiction is like a spider's web, attached ever so lightly perhaps, but still attached to life at all four corners … when the web is pulled askew, hooked up at the edge, torn in the middle, one remembers that these webs are not spun in mid-air by incorporeal creatures, but are the work of suffering human beings, and are attached to grossly material things, like health and money and the houses we live in.

[Judith Shakespeare]
… it would have been impossible, completely and entirely, for any woman to have written the plays of Shakespeare in the age of Shakespeare. Let me imagine, since facts are so hard to come by, what would have happened had Shakespeare had a wonderfully gifted sister, called Judith, let us say. Shakespeare himself went, very probably – his mother was an heiress – to the grammar school, where he may have learnt Latin – Ovid, Virgil, and Horace – and the elements of grammar and logic. He was, it is well known, a wild boy who poached rabbits, perhaps shot a deer, and had, rather sooner than he should have done, to marry a woman in the neighbourhood, who bore him a child rather quicker than was right. That escapade sent him to seek his fortune in London. He had, it seemed, a taste for the theatre; he began by holding horses at the stage door. Very soon he got work in the theatre, became a successful actor, and lived at the hub of the universe, meeting everybody, knowing everybody, practising his art on the boards, exercising his wits in the streets, and even getting access to the palace of the queen. Meanwhile his extraordinarily gifted sister, let us suppose, remained at home. She was as adventurous, as imaginative, as agog to see the world as he was. But she was not sent to school. She had no chance of learning grammar and logic, let alone

of reading Horace and Virgil. She picked up a book now and then, one of her brother's perhaps, and read a few pages. But then her parents came in and told her to mend the stocking or mind the stew and not moon about with books and papers. They would have spoken sharply but kindly, for they were substantial people who knew the conditions of life for a woman and loved their daughter – indeed, more likely than not she was the apple of her father's eye. Perhaps she scribbled some pages up in an apple loft on the sly, but she was careful to hide them or set fire to them. Soon, however, before was out of her teens, she was to be betrothed to the son of a neighbouring wool-stapler. She cried out that marriage was hateful to her, and for that she was severely beaten by her father. Then he ceased to scold her. He begged her instead not to hurt him, not to shame him in this matter of her marriage. He would give her a chain of beads or a fine petticoat, he said; and there were tears in his eyes. How could she disobey him? How could she break his heart? The force of her own gift alone drove her to it. She made up a small parcel of her belongings, let herself down by a rope one summer's night and took the road to London. She was not seventeen. The birds that sang in the hedge were not more musical than she was. She had the quickest fancy, a gift like her brother's, for the tune of words. Like him, she had a taste for the theatre. She stood at the stage door; she wanted to act, she said. Men laughed in her face. The manager – a fat, loose-lipped man – guffawed. He bellowed something about poodles dancing and women acting – no woman, he said, could possibly be an actress. He hinted – you can imagine what. She could get no training in her craft. Could she even seek her dinner in a tavern or roam the streets at midnight? Yet her genius was for fiction and lusted to feed abundantly upon the lives of men and women and the study of their ways. At last – for she was very young, oddly like Shakespeare the poet in her face, with the same grey eyes and rounded brows – at last Nick Greene the actor-manager took pity on her; she found herself with child by that gentleman and so – who shall measure the heat and violence of the poet's heart when caught and tangled in a woman's body? – killed herself one winter's night and lies buried at some cross-roads where the omnibuses now stop outside the Elephant and Castle.

Sigmund Freud

From 'Femininity' (1933)

> ... Undoubtedly the material is different to start with in boys and girls; it did not need psychoanalysis to establish that ... Both sexes [however]

seem to pass through the early phases of ... development in the same manner ... We are now obliged to recognize that the little girl is a little man ... Unless we can find something that is specific for girls and is not present or not in the same way present in boys, we shall not have explained the termination of the attachment of girls to their mother.

I believe we have found this specific factor, and indeed where we expected to find it, even though in a surprising form. Where we expected to find it, I say, for it lies in the castration complex. After all, the anatomical distinction [between the sexes] must express itself in psychical consequences. It was, however, a surprise to learn from analyses that girls hold their mother responsible for their lack of a penis and do not forgive her for their being thus put at a disadvantage ...

... The castration complex of girls is also started by the sight of the genitals of the other sex. They at once notice the difference and, it must be admitted, its significance too. They feel seriously wronged, often declare that they want to 'have something like it too', and fall victim to 'envy for the penis', which will leave ineradicable traces on their development and the formation of their character ... The girl's recognition of the fact of her being without a penis does not by any means imply that she submits to the fact easily ... The wish to get the longed-for penis eventually in spite of everything may contribute to the motives that drive a mature woman to analysis, and what she may reasonably expect from analysis – a capacity, for instance, to carry on an intellectual profession– may often be recognized as a sublimated modification of this repressed wish ...

The discovery that she is castrated is a turning-point in a girl's growth. Three possible lines of development start from it: one leads to sexual inhibition or to neurosis, the second to change of character in the sense of a masculinity complex, the third, finally, to normal femininity ... By this [masculinity complex] we mean that the girl refuses, as it were, to recognise the unwelcome fact and, defiantly rebellious, even exaggerates her previous masculinity ...

... Thus, we attribute a larger amount of narcissism to femininity, which also affects women's choice of object, so that to be loved is a stronger need for them than to love. The effect of penis-envy has a share, further, in the physical vanity of women, since they are bound to value their charms more highly as a late compensation for their original sexual inferiority. Shame, which is considered to be a feminine characteristic *par excellence* but is far more a matter of convention than might be supposed, has as its purpose, we believe, concealment of genital deficiency ...

The fact that women must be regarded as having little sense of justice is no doubt related to the predominance of envy in their mental life; for the demand for justice is a modification of envy ...

... But do not forget that I have only been describing women in so far as their nature is determined by their sexual function. It is true that that influence extends very far; but we do not overlook the fact that an individual woman may be a human being in other respects as well. If you want to know more about femininity, inquire from your own experiences of life, or turn to the poets ...

Stevie Smith

'Papa Love Baby' (1937)

Papa Love Baby
My mother was a romantic girl
So she had to marry a man with his hair in curl
Who subsequently became my unrespected papa,
But that was a long time ago now.

What folly it is that daughters are always supposed to be
In love with papa. It wasn't the case with me
I couldn't take to him at all.
But he took to me
What a sad fate to befall
A child of three.
I sat upright in my baby carriage
And wished mama hadn't made such a foolish marriage.
I tried to hide it, but it showed in my eyes unfortunately
And a fortnight later papa ran away to sea.

He used to come home on leave
It was always the same
I could not grieve
But I think I was somewhat to blame.

Phyllis McGinley

'The 5:32' (1951)

The 5:32
She said, If tomorrow my world were torn in two,
Blacked out, dissolved, I think I would remember
(As if transfixed in unsurrendering amber)
This hour best of all the hours I knew:

When cars came backing into the shabby station,
Children scuffing the seats, and the women driving
With ribbons around their hair, and the trains arriving,
And the men getting off with tired but practiced motion.

Yes, I would remember my life like this, she said:
Autumn, the platform red with Virginia creeper,
And a man coming toward me, smiling, the evening paper
Under his arm, and his hat pushed back on his head,
And wood smoke lying like haze on the quiet town,
And dinner waiting, and the sun not yet gone down.

Sylvia Plath

'Ode for Ted' (21 April 1956); 'Wuthering Heights' (September 1961)

Ode for Ted
From under crunch of my man's boot
green oat-sprouts jut;
he names a lapwing, starts rabbits in a rout
legging it most nimble
to sprigged hedge of bramble,
stalks red fox, shrewd stoat.

Loam-humps, he says, moles shunt
up from delved worm-haunt;
blue fur, moles have; hefting chalk-hulled flint
he with rock splits open
knobbed quartz; flayed colors ripen
rich, brown, sudden in sunglint.

For his least look, scant acres yield:
each finger-furrowed field
heaves forth stalk, leaf, fruit-nubbed emerald;
bright grain sprung so rarely
he hauls to his will early;
at his hand's staunch hest, birds build.

Ringdoves roost well within his wood,
shirr songs to suit which mood
he saunters in; how but most glad
could be this adam's woman
when all earth his words do summon
leaps to laud such man's blood!

Wuthering Heights
The horizons ring me like faggots,
Tilted and disparate, and always unstable.
Touched by a match, they might warm me,
And their fine lines singe
The air to orange
Before the distances they pin evaporate,
Weighting the pale sky with a solider color.
But they only dissolve and dissolve
Like a series of promises, as I step forward.

There is no life higher than the grasstops
Or the hearts of sheep, and the wind
Pours by like destiny, bending
Everything in one direction.
I can feel it trying
To funnel my heat away.
If I pay the roots of the heather
Too close attention, they will invite me
To whiten my bones among them.

The sheep know where they are,
Browsing in their dirty wool-clouds,
Gray as the weather.
The black slots of their pupils take me in.
It is like being mailed into space,
A thin, silly message.
They stand about in grandmotherly disguise,
All wig curls and yellow teeth
And hard, marbly baas.

I come to wheel ruts, and water
Limpid as the solitudes
That flee through my fingers.
Hollow doorsteps go from grass to grass;
Lintel and sill have unhinged themselves.
Of people the air only
Remembers a few odd syllables.
It rehearses them moaningly:
Black stone, black stone.

The sky leans on me, me, the one upright
Among all horizontals.
The grass is beating its head distractedly.
It is too delicate
For a life in such company;
Darkness terrifies it.
Now, in valleys narrow
And black as purses, the house lights
Gleam like small change.

Toni Morrison

From *The Bluest Eye* (1970)

The three women sat talking about various miseries they had had,
their cure or abatement, what had helped …

But they had been young once. The odor of their armpits and
haunches had mingled into a lovely musk; their eyes had been furtive,
their lips relaxed, and the delicate turn of their heads on those slim
black necks had been like nothing other than a doe's. Their laughter
had been more touch than sound.

Then they had grown. Edging into life from the back door.
Becoming. Everybody in the world was in a position to give them
orders. White women said, 'Do this.' White children said, 'Give me
that.' White men said, 'Come here.' Black men said, 'Lay down.' The
only people they need not take orders from were black children and
each other. But they took all of that and re-created it in their own
image. They ran the houses of white people, and knew it. When white
men beat their men, they cleaned up the blood and went home to
receive abuse from the victim. They beat their children with one hand
and stole for them with the other. The hands that felled trees also cut
umbilical cords; the hands that wrung the necks of chickens and
butchered hogs also nudged African violets into bloom; the arms that
loaded sheaves, bales, and sacks rocked babies into sleep. They patted

| WOMEN'S WRITING: PAST AND PRESENT

biscuits into flaky ovals of innocence – and shrouded the dead. They plowed all day and came home to nestle like plums under the limbs of their men. The legs that straddled a mule's back were the same ones that straddled their men's hips. And the difference was all the difference there was.

Then they were old. Their bodies honed, their odor sour. Squatting in a cane field, stooping in a cotton field, kneeling by a river bank, they had carried a world on their heads. They had given over the lives of their own children and tendered their grandchildren. With relief they wrapped their heads in rags, and their breasts in flannel; eased their feet into felt. They were through with lust and lactation, beyond tears and terror. They alone could walk the roads of Mississippi, the lanes of Georgia, the fields of Alabama unmolested. They were old enough to be irritable when and where they chose, tired enough to look forward to death, disinterested enough to accept the idea of pain while ignoring the presence of pain. They were, in fact and at last, free.

Erica Jong

'Alcestis on the Poetry Circuit' (1973); from *Fanny* (1980)

Alcestis on the Poetry Circuit
(IN MEMORIAM Marina Tsvetayeva [Russian poet, 1892–1941], Anna Wickham [English poet, 1884–1947], Sylvia Plath, Shakespeare's sister, etc., etc.)

The best slave
does not need to be beaten.
She beats herself.

Not with a leather whip,
or with sticks and twigs,
not with a blackjack
or a billyclub,
but with the fine whip
of her own tongue
& the subtle beating
of her mind
against her mind.

For who can hate her half so well
as she hates herself?
& who can match the finesse
of her self-abuse?

Years of training
are required for this.
Twenty years
of subtle self-indulgence,
self-denial;
until the subject
thinks herself a queen
& yet a beggar –
both at the same time.
She must doubt herself
in everything but love.

She must choose passionately
& badly.
She must feel lost as a dog
without her master.
She must refer all moral questions
to her mirror.
She must fall in love with a cossack
or a poet.

She must never go out of the house
unless veiled in paint.
She must wear tight shoes
so she always remembers her bondage.
She must never forget
she is rooted in the ground.

Though she is quick to learn
& admittedly clever,
her natural doubt of herself
should make her so weak
that she dabbles brilliantly
in half a dozen talents
& thus embellishes
but does not change
our life.

If she's an artist
& comes close to genius,
the very fact of her gift
should cause her such pain
that she will take her own life
rather than best us.

& after she dies, we will cry
& make her a saint.

From Fanny

'I was just this Moment wond'ring,' I said, the Blood flying up into my Face, Neck, and Breasts, 'if I might pose you a few Queries concerning the Art of Poesy.'

'Pose all you like, my Dear,' says he, loping o'er to the Bed, and seating himself upon the edge of it, whence his tiny Legs dangl'd like broken Twigs in the Wind, after a Storm.

'Well, then,' said I, so engross'd in my Thoughts of the Muses that I scarce troubl'd to inquire what he was doing in my Chamber, 'is it vain for a Woman to wish to be a Poet, or e'en to be the first Female Laureate someday?'

Whereupon he broke into a Gale of unkind Laughter, which made me blush still harder for my presum'd Foolishness.

'Fanny, my Dear, the Answer is implied in the Query itself. Men are Poets; Women are meant to be their Muses upon Earth. You are the Inspiration of the Poems, not the Creator of Poems, and why should you wish it otherwise?'

I confess I was dumbfounded by the Manner in which he pos'd his Query and press'd his Point. I had my own tentative first Verses secreted directly 'neath the Pillow of the Bed, but I was far too abash'd at that Moment to draw 'em out and ask his Opinion. I'faith, with each Word he utter'd, I was coming, increasingly, to disdain those Verses, which only a few Moments before had seem'd touch'd with the Fire of the Muses.

'See these fine twin Globes?' said the Poet, suddenly reaching into my Boddice and disengaging my Breasts. I gasp'd with Shock but dar'd not interrupt the Poet's Flow of beauteous Words ... For tho' I found his Person loath-some, his Words were fine and elegant, and despite what he argu'd about the Fair Sex and the Art of Poetry, I was e're more conquer'd by fine Language than by Fine Looks.

'But, Sir,' I protested, moving, albeit momentarily, out of his Grasp, 'is not Inspiration a Thing which hath no Gender, is neither male nor female, as Angels are neither male nor female?'

'In Theory, that is correct,' said the Poet, reaching under my Shift ... 'but in Practice, Inspiration more frequently visits those of the Male Sex, and for this following Reason, mark you well. As the Muse is female, so the Muse is more likely to receive male Lovers than female ones. Therefore, a Woman Poet is an Absurdity of Nature, a vile, despis'd Creature whose Fate must e'er be Loneliness, Melancholy, Despair, and eventually Self-Slaughter. Howe'er, if she chooses the sensible Path, and devotes her whole Life to serving a Poet of the Masculine Gender, the Gods shall bless her, and all the

Universe resound with her Praise. 'Tis all Part of Nature's Great Plan. As Angels are above Men and God is above Angels, so Women are below Men and above Children and Dogs; but if Women seek to upset that Great Order by usurping Men in their proper Position of Superiority, both in the Arts and the Sciences, as well as Politicks, Society, and Marriage, they reap nothing but Chaos and Anarchy, and i'faith the whole World tumbles to its Ruin ...'

'But Sir,' I said, above the growing Pounding of my Blood in my Ears, like Waves upon the Shore, 'cannot this Plan be alter'd? Cannot a Great Female Poet rise up who will give the Lye to these immutable Theories?'

'No,' said the Poet, 'a thousand Times NO. For whate'er exists in Nature is but an Expression of God's Will, and if He hath placed Women below Men, you can be sure 'tis for a Noble Purpose. In short, whate'er is, IS RIGHT.'

Whereupon he loosen'd his Breeches ... and stood ready to assault my Maidenhead.

Adrienne Rich

'Twenty-One Love Poems: XIII' (1974–1976); from 'Foreword' to *On Lies, Secrets, and Silence: Selected Prose, 1966–1978* (1979); from 'Compulsory Heterosexuality and Lesbian Existence' (1980)

Twenty-One Love Poems: XIII
The rules break like a thermometer,
quicksilver spills across the charted systems,
we're out in a country that has no language
no laws, we're chasing the raven and the wren
through gorges unexplored since dawn
whatever we do together is pure invention
the maps they gave us were out of date
by years ... we're driving through the desert
wondering if the water will hold out
the hallucinations turn to simple villages
the music on the radio comes clear—
neither *Rosenkavalier nor Götterdämmerung*
but a woman's voice singing old songs
with new words, with a quiet bass, a flute
plucked and fingered by women outside the law.

From 'Foreword' to On Lies, Secrets, and Silence: Selected Prose, 1966–1978

The entire history of women's struggle for self-determination has been muffled in silence over and over. One serious cultural obstacle encountered by any feminist writer is that each feminist work has tended to be received as if it emerged from nowhere; as if each of us had lived, thought, and worked without any historical past or contextual present. This is one of the ways in which women's work and thinking has been made to seem sporadic, errant, orphaned of any tradition of its own.

From 'Compulsory Heterosexuality and Lesbian Existence'

Characteristics of male power include *the power of men ... to cramp their* [women's] *creativeness* [through] ... witch persecutions as campaigns against midwives and female healers, and as pogrom against independent, 'unassimilated' women; definition of male pursuits as more valuable than female within any culture, so that cultural values become the embodiment of male subjectivity; restriction of female self-fulfillment to marriage and motherhood; sexual exploitation of women by male artists and teachers; the social and economic disruption of women's creative aspirations; erasure of female tradition ...

Margaret Atwood

'Spelling' (1981); from *The Blind Assassin* (2000); from 'Introduction: Into the labyrinth' from *Negotiating with the Dead: A Writer on Writing* (2002)

Spelling

My daughter plays on the floor
with plastic letters,
red, blue & hard yellow,
learning how to spell,
spelling,
how to make spells

*   *   *   *   *   *   *   *

and I wonder how many women
denied themselves daughters,
closed themselves in rooms,
drew the curtains
so they could mainline words.

*   *   *   *   *   *   *   *

A child is not a poem,
a poem is not a child.
There is no either/or.
However.

*   *   *   *   *   *   *   *

I return to the story
of the woman caught in the war
& in labor, her thighs tied
together by the enemy
so she could not give birth.

Ancestress: the burning witch,
her mouth covered by leather
to strangle words.

A word after a word
after a word is power.

*   *   *   *   *   *   *   *

At the point where language falls away
from the hot bones, at the point
where the rock breaks open and darkness
flows out of it like blood, at
the melting point of granite
when the bones know
they are hollow & the word
splits & doubles & speaks
the truth & the body
itself becomes a mouth.

This is a metaphor.

*   *   *   *   *   *   *   *

How do you learn to spell?
Blood, sky & the sun,
your own name first,
your first naming, your first name,
your first word.

From* The Blind Assassin *(2000)

The Toronto Star, May 26, 1945
QUESTIONS RAISED IN CITY DEATH
SPECIAL TO THE STAR

A coroner's inquest has returned a verdict of accidental death in last week's St. Clair Ave. fatality. Miss Laura Chase, 25, was travelling west on the afternoon of May 18 when her car swerved through the barriers protecting a repair site on the bridge and crashed into the ravine below, catching fire. Miss Chase was killed instantly. Her sister, Mrs. Richard E. Griffen, wife of the prominent manufacturer, gave evidence that Miss Chase suffered from severe headaches affecting her vision. In reply to questioning, she denied any possibility of intoxication as Miss Chase did not drink.

It was the police view that a tire caught in an exposed streetcar track was a contributing factor. Questions were raised as to the adequacy of safety precautions taken by the City, but after expert testimony by City engineer Gordon Perkins these were dismissed.

The accident has occasioned renewed protests over the state of the streetcar tracks on this stretch of roadway. Mr. Herb T. Jolliffe, representing local ratepayers, told Star reporters that this was not the first mishap caused by neglected tracks. City Council should take note.

From 'Introduction: Into the labyrinth' from* Negotiating with the Dead: A Writer on Writing *(2002)

This book … is about writing, although it isn't about how to write; nor is it about my own writing; nor is it about the writing of any person or age or country in particular. How to describe it? Let's say it's about the position the writer finds himself in; or herself, which is always a little different. It's the sort of book a person who's been laboring in the wordmines for, say, forty years – by coincidence, roughly the time I myself have been doing this – the book such a person might think of beginning, the day after he or she wakes up in the middle of the night and wonders what she's been up to all this time.

What has she been up to, and why, and for whom? And what is this *writing* anyway, as a human activity or as a vocation, or as a profession, or as a hack job, or perhaps even as an art, and why do so many people feel compelled to do it? In what ways is it different from – for instance – painting or composing or singing or dancing or acting? And how have other people who have done this thing viewed their own activity, and themselves in relation to it? And are their views any comfort? And has the concept of the writer *qua* writer, as expounded by (of course) writers, changed at all over the years? And what exactly do we mean when we say *writer*? What sort of creature do we have in mind? Is the writer the unacknowledged legislator of the world, as [English Romantic poet Percy Bysshe] Shelley so grandiosely proclaimed, or is he one of [the nineteenth-century Scottish philosopher Thomas] Carlyle's blimp-like Great Men, or is he the snivelling neurotic wreck and ineffectual weenie so beloved of his contemporary biographers?

Obstruction, obscurity, emptiness, disorientation, twilight, blackout, often combined with a struggle or path or journey – an inability to see one's way forward, but a feeling that there was a way forward, and that the act of going forward would eventually bring about the conditions for vision – these were the common elements [I found] in many descriptions of the process of writing. I was reminded of something a medical student said to me about the interior of the human body, forty years ago: 'It's dark in there.'

Possibly, then, writing has to do with darkness, and a desire or perhaps a compulsion to enter it, and, with luck, to illuminate it, and to bring something back out to the light. This book is about that kind of darkness, and that kind of desire.

Emily Grosholz

'Ithaka' (2002)

Ithaka
Penelope held off her ravenous suitors
by promising, tomorrow and tomorrow,
she'd finish lost Ulysses' winding sheet.
The Greek text says that she composed in light,

and analyzed in darkness. Women figures
unravelled are not quite analysis,
rather a woman trying to understand
the altitude and basis of her island.

All day Penelope addressed the warp,
her shuttle a small craft with two directions.
All night her solitude relit the torch.
To analyze is to set life in question,

despite the crush of suitors at the door,
the cold synthetic wave raking the shore.

Carol Ann Duffy

'Anon' (2002); 'White Writing' (2002)

Anon

If she were here
she'd forget who she was,
it's been so long,
maybe a nurse, a nanny,
maybe a nun –
Anon.

A girl I met
was willing to bet
that she still lived on –
Anon –
but had packed it all in,
the best verb, the right noun,
for a life in the sun.

A woman I knew
kept her skull
on a shelf in a room –
Anon's –
and swore that one day
as she worked at her desk
it cleared its throat
as though it had something
to get off its chest.

But I know best –
how she passed on her pen
like a baton
down through the years,
with a hey nonny
hey nonny
hey nonny no –
Anon.

White Writing

No vows written to wed you,
I write them white,
my lips on yours,
light in the soft hours of our married years.

No prayers written to bless you,
I write them white,
your soul a flame,
bright in the window of your maiden name.

No laws written to guard you,
I write them white,
your hand in mine,
palm against palm, lifeline, heartline.

No rules written to guide you,
I write them white,
words on the wind,
traced with a stick where we walk on the sand.

No news written to tell you,
I write it white,
foam on a wave
as we lift up our skirts in the sea, wade,

see last gold sun behind clouds,
inked water in moonlight.
No poems written to praise you,
I write them white.

Critical approaches

Part 4 considers the range of critical responses you may find useful in developing your own ideas.

- How does women's writing fit into cultural and literary history?

- How do women writers regard their own work?

- How has the response to specific writers and texts changed over time?

Different reactions during different eras

Commenting on the proportion of women represented in the *New Dictionary of National Biography* (Project Update, Autumn 2002), the editor, Brian Harrison, notes that 'the dictionary's content inevitably reflects past attitudes, and until very recently femininity was thought to require reticence, except at the highest social levels'. Focusing specifically on women poets, the literary critic Paula Bennett discusses this issue further in *My Life a Loaded Gun: Female Creativity and Feminist Poetics* (1986):

> Lacking the male poet's long-established tradition of self-exploration and self-validation, women poets in our culture have been torn between restrictive definitions of what a woman is and their own fears of being or seeming unwomanly. As a result, they have been unable to allow the full truth of their experience to empower their speaking voice. Without predecessors to whom they might appeal or upon whom they might model themselves, they have either fit into the existing masculinist tradition, or they have worked within a subcultural tradition of their own – the literature of the 'poetess'. In either case, they have inevitably been led *to disassociate the concept of creative power from their woman selves*. Though often possessed ... of extraordinary gifts, they have rarely felt these gifts as inherently theirs.

Bennett argues that for the woman writer 'to exercise her creativity to its fullest, she must first be able to heal the internal divisions that have historically distorted and controlled her relationship to her craft ... But for her to arrive at this self-acceptance, she must possess a definition of her womanhood that is broad enough, flexible enough, to encompass all that she actually is.'

Reading and rereading specific writers and texts

Virginia Woolf in *A Room of One's Own* sees Jane Eyre as struggling with the conflict Bennett describes: longing for freedom, she is well aware that she may be considered 'unwomanly'.

▶ Look closely at the passage from *Jane Eyre* in Part 1, pages 45–46. To what degree does Charlotte Brontë seem to you to be declaring her feminist convictions here rather than writing a novel? Are the two impulses – angry argument and the writing of fiction – in conflict?

Woolf felt that such anger was an impediment to artistic expression. Praising Brontë as a woman of 'genius', Woolf declares that her 'indignation' prevents her from expressing that genius 'whole and entire'. Indeed, until Charlotte Brontë and the woman writer more generally is able to avoid such anger – that is, until the world changes – 'Her books will be deformed and twisted. She will write in a rage where she should write calmly. She will write foolishly where she should write wisely. She will write of herself where she should write of her characters. She is at war with her lot. How could she help but die young, cramped and thwarted?'

Woolf develops her ideas further in her essay 'Women and Fiction' (1929), writing that in George Eliot's *Middlemarch* (1872) as in *Jane Eyre*:

> … we are conscious not merely of the writer's character, as we are conscious of the character of Charles Dickens, but we are conscious of a woman's presence — of someone resenting the treatment of her sex and pleading for its rights. This brings into women's writing an element which is entirely absent from a man's, unless, indeed, he happens to be a working man or a negro, or one who for some other reason is conscious of disability. It introduces a distortion and is frequently the cause of weakness. The desire to plead some personal cause or to make a character the mouthpiece of some personal discontent or grievance always has a distressing effect, as if the spot at which the reader's attention is directed were suddenly twofold instead of single.
> The genius of Jane Austen and Emily Brontë is never more convincing than in their power to ignore such claims and solicitations …

▶ Do you agree with Woolf? How do Woolf's standards, which depend on her own ideas about the woman writer in Britain in the 1920s, help you to understand the work of women writers you have read? What roles do you feel anger and the woman writer's own life experiences play, for example, in poems by Emily Dickinson or Erica Jong? In fiction by such women writers as Kate Chopin or Toni Morrison? You might look at the poems and prose extracts by these writers which appear in Part 3, pages 88–91, 101–104, 92–93 and 100–101; an additional poem by Jong appears in Part 5, pages 116–118.

The English cultural critic and novelist Jeanette Winterson (b. 1960) has written admiringly about Virginia Woolf in *Art Objects: Essays on Ecstasy and Effrontery* (1995), a book in which she also reflects on the role of anger in women's writing. The title of her book is a play on words: 'art objects' usually means 'objects of art', but Winterson has stated that in this case she is using 'objects' as a verb to say what she thinks art does or ought to do.

The author of several novels, including *Oranges are Not the Only Fruit* (1984) and *Sexing the Cherry* (1989), Winterson directs her objections in *Art Objects* towards many targets, among them the current tendency to reduce a piece of writing to the biography of the author or the autobiographical elements that may appear in a text. She argues that art should be able to stand apart from the particularities of a writer's life. She begins her essay 'The Semiotics of Sex' with this anecdote:

> I was in a bookshop recently when a young woman approached me. She told me she was writing an essay on my work and that of Radclyffe Hall [the conflicted lesbian author who wrote *The Well of Loneliness* in 1928]. Could I help?
> 'Yes,' I said, 'Our work has nothing in common.'
> 'I thought you were a lesbian.' she said.

What does this anecdote suggest about Winterson's view of the relation between a writer's life and her work? What does it suggest about her view of the tradition of women's writing? Winterson concludes her essay with another anecdote:

> I was in a bookshop recently and a young man came up to me and said 'Is *Sexing the Cherry* a reading of [T.S. Eliot's] *Four Quartets?*'
> 'Yes' I said, and he kissed me.

What is Winterson saying here about the place of women writers within the literary canon? What do her anecdotes reveal about the differences between her era and Woolf's? Specifically, what do Winterson's anecdotes reveal about how reading women writers as well as women's writing itself has changed during the course of the 20th century?

Winterson concludes *Art Objects* by evoking Woolf very specifically. In the final essay, 'A Work of My Own', Winterson describes the struggles she has confronted as what she calls 'an experimenter' in literature. She writes, 'The challenge is exhilarating and enviable.' As you read the following passage, consider what Winterson gains by recalling Woolf in both her diction and her rhythms. You might also consider what Winterson is implying here about the tradition of women writers, past and present, even as she emphasises her own unique voice and what she sees as her very contemporary subject matter and audience:

> The true writer will have to build up her readership from among those who still want to read and who want more than the glories of the past nicely reproduced. I have been able to build a readership, largely through a young student population, who want my books on their courses and by their beds. Reading is sexy.
> They know it is. They know that there is such a thing as art and that it is not interchangeable with the word 'entertainment'. They do not care for maundering middle-class middle-aged elegies. Judge the

work not the writer seems to be what a new generation is prepared to do. It is for a new generation that I write.

Assignments

1 Consider the following statement by the literary scholar Mary Joannou in her book *Contemporary Women's Writing* (2000):

> The insistence on purely literary criteria for determining which works of fiction should be studied and taught runs the risk of leaving us with only a handful of writers ... whose stature as writers of world importance ... could not be disputed. But the elevation of the political by itself as a criteria of value in opposition to the literary carries the danger of undervaluing the importance of the pleasures of the text and the very reasons why we turn to literary work rather than to sociology, politics or history in the first place; i.e. the interaction between ideas, language and imagery which accounts for the pleasure of discovering our feelings, values and beliefs expressed imaginatively in fictional form.

According to Joannou, what is the problem facing the contemporary reader of women's writing? Choose a specific text and define its literary value in light of Joannou's statement.

2 In *Becoming a Heroine* (1982), the literary critic Rachel Brownstein examines novels written by both women and men. She concludes that 'classic' English novels 'do not begin to offer a blueprint for a feminist utopia; on the contrary, to enjoy them is to experience the pull of a seductive, reactionary dream'. You might begin to think about this statement by considering Brownstein's language: what is the difference between 'a blueprint for a feminist utopia' and 'a seductive, reactionary dream'? What is Brownstein suggesting about how and even why women and men read literature? How does her conclusion help you to understand a particular text by either a male or a female writer? Do the women writers you have read challenge Brownstein by offering an alternative vision of what it means to be a 'heroine' in a literary text?

How to write about women writers

Part 5 considers the task of writing about literature by women.

- Where do I start? What sort of text am I dealing with?

- What can I learn from comparing one literary work with another?

- What can I say about the context in which a text was written and in which it may be read?

- How can I evaluate the views of other readers to help me clarify my own point of view?

Establishing the context

When writing about literature written by women, it is possible to approach from a number of different directions. You can choose to develop a reading of a specific work in terms of a fairly narrow context (for instance, another work by the same author) or within a much wider context (for instance, other works written by male or female contemporaries or the author's own life). Particular works and authors seem to encourage some approaches rather than others, but it is important to begin with an examination of the work itself – although you may later decide that a direct discussion of the work can only come after a specific context has been established. Basic questions to ask about a literary work might include:

- What is this work about, what is the story (if it has one), what is the subject?

- What is the woman writer saying, what is the work's main idea or theme?

- What are the author's values? How does she want the reader to feel about the work?

- How does the woman writer do it – convey facts or feelings or ideas or values? What literary techniques operate to make readers respond as they do?

Writing about literature written by women involves considering these questions within an historical and cultural context. For example:

- In what ways does this work or author engage with subjects, settings, language and issues that reflect her time and place, her class and even her nationality?

- How does the author draw on contemporary or past attitudes and values in terms of her material and themes?

- In what ways are the literary techniques in the text new and individual? In what ways are they experimental? In what ways do they reflect the traditions of earlier writing and thinking?

- How is this text similar to or different from other earlier or contemporary texts by women or by men?

Such challenging questions help you to look carefully not at single works or individual women writers in isolation, but to consider them in comparison with other works and authors. These contextualising questions also encourage you to look at other readers' responses.

Reading Colette

In *Colette, Beauvoir, and Duras: Age and Women Writers* (1999), her study of three French women writers, Bethany Ladimer asserts that 'What is true of aging women writers in France is true for women writers everywhere.' Specifically, Sidonie-Gabrielle Claudine Colette (1873–1954), Simone de Beauvoir (1908–1986) and Marguerite Duras (1914–1996) were all 'genuinely transgressive in their respective times'. Ladimer argues that, in part because of the maturity she achieved in old age, Colette was able to achieve a 'feminine identity that could not be contained within, or lay *beyond*, French traditional definitions of femininity and the silence or echo of male desire'. Such traditions, this scholar indicates, were based on 'courtship, sexual relationships, and childbearing'.

How can we use Ladimer's assertions about Colette? How do her statements help us to understand Colette's work or the work of other women writers? In 'Dear Colette' (1975), her tribute to this writer, Erica Jong responds to the ideas Ladimer explores. Contextualising Colette in terms of her long and varied life, Jong suggests in this poem why she finds Colette important. Jong's text thus offers us a critical reading of the women writers she cites as well as an original poem, for it suggests critical ways of thinking about her subject at the same time that it reveals the personality and values of its speaker.

Dear Colette

Dear Colette,
I want to write to you
about being a woman
for that is what
you write to me.

I want to tell you how your face
enduring after thirty, forty, fifty …
hangs above my desk
like my own muse.

I want to tell you how your hands
reach out from your books
& seize my heart.

I want to tell you how your hair
electrifies my thoughts
like my own halo.

I want to tell you how your eyes
penetrate my fear
& make it melt.

I want to tell you
simply that I love you –
though you are 'dead'
& I am still 'alive'.

Suicides & spinsters –
all our kind!
Even decorous Jane Austen
never marrying,
& Sappho leaping,
& Sylvia in the oven,
& Anna Wickham, Tsvetaeva, Sara Teasdale,
& pale Virginia floating like Ophelia,
& Emily alone, alone, alone …

But you endure & marry,
go on writing,
lose a husband, gain a husband,
go on writing,
sing & tap dance
& you go on writing,
have a child and still
you go on writing,
love a woman, love a man
& go on writing.
You endure your writing
& your life.

Dear Colette,
I only want to thank you:

for your eyes ringed
with bluest paint like bruises,
for your hair gathering sparks
like brush fire,
for your hands which never willingly
let go,
for your years, your child, your lovers,
all your books ...

Dear Colette,
you hold me
to this life.

What do you think Jong means here when she speaks of women writers as 'Suicides &
spinsters'? Reflecting on the lives and work of the women writers you have read, you
may find many 'old maids' and early deaths; what is gained here by Jong's emphasis
on these elements? Why does Jong entitle her poem 'Dear Colette'? Why does Jong
thank Colette? On the one hand, Jong considers Colette as someone very 'dear' to her
– she even hangs a picture of Colette on her study wall as inspiration – but on the
other hand 'Dear Colette' also suggests that Jong's poem is a kind of a letter to Colette.
Genre has historically been an issue in women's writing, and certainly Jong raises the
issue in 'Dear Colette' by her direct address.

In thinking further about this poem, you might want to find out more
biographical information about the writer Colette. Because Jong is so specific in
her description of Colette's life and appearance, you might also want to look at
some of the many photographs of this author. The web is an excellent source for
this information. You may want to look as well for images (reproduced from
photographs or paintings) of the other women Jong and Ladimer mention; you
might even look for pictures of Jong herself. What information do these images
add to the contexts which help you to understand these particular authors?

In considering how to write about women writers, you might finally consider
how to read the last lines of 'Dear Colette': 'you hold me / to this life.' When critics
such as Ladimer and writers such as Jong examine the tradition of women's
writing, stressing particular elements or perhaps, as in Jong's case, situating
themselves within that tradition, they present us with a fresh way of reading
literature, asking us to rethink conventional literary canons and to reflect on our
own values in the process of understanding whatever texts we read.

Assignments

1   Many women writers have examined the subject of courtship in their writing. Look at several texts by authors from different periods and/or countries. You might examine, for instance, works by Sappho, Murasaki, Aphra Behn, Jane Austen, Charlotte Brontë, Edith Wharton, May Sinclair, Zora Neale Hurston, Mary McCarthy, Alice Walker, Ruth Prawer Jhabvala, Margaret Atwood or Erica Jong. What is at stake in courtship for both male and female characters? What are the conventions and rituals of the courtship? Do the characters follow or break these 'rules'? What sorts of power do the women have and how do they use it? What is the author's view of her characters' behaviour and how do you know?

2   Consider the figure of the mad woman in several texts. You might look, for instance, at Charlotte Brontë's *Jane Eyre* (1847), Charlotte Perkins Gilman's short story 'The Yellow Wallpaper' (1892), Sylvia Plath's *The Bell Jar* (1963) Joanne Greenburg's *I Never Promised You a Rose Garden* (1964), Marilyn French's *The Women's Room* (1977), Doris Lessing's short story 'To Room Nineteen' (1978), Janet Frame's *An Angel at My Table* (1984) or Alice Walker's *Possessing the Secret of Joy* (1992). What seems to drive these female characters 'over the edge'? Are we supposed to sympathise or disapprove of these characters? Are they essentially different or similar to the other characters in their texts? How does the author use a mad woman to develop her plot and convey her themes?

3   Look at several texts written by women in the first person. You might look at works by Queen Elizabeth I, Anne Finch, Mary Wollstonecraft, Emily Dickinson, Elizabeth Barrett Browning, Sylvia Plath, or Adrienne Rich. What differences and similarities do you find among the speakers? What is gained – or lost – by the author's use of this point of view? What are the advantages and what are the limitations of this perspective? What is the effect on the reader of the first-person speaker? In what ways does the period in which the author wrote help you to understand her choice of a first-person point of view?

4   In *Writing Beyond the Ending* (1985), Rachel Blau Duplessis contends that many women's fictions traditionally end with a woman's marriage. In what ways is marriage the 'end' of a woman's story? Consider, for instance, the endings of Jane Austen's *Pride and Prejudice* (1813),

Charlotte Brontë's *Jane Eyre* (1847) or Edith Wharton's *The Age of Innocence* (1920). In what ways – especially for modern, feminist writers – is marriage merely the beginning of the story? You might consider Kate Chopin's *The Awakening* (1899) Edith Wharton's *The Custom of the Country* (1913), H.D.'s *Bid Me to Live* (1960), Marilyn French's *The Women's Room* (1977) or Anne Tyler's *Ladder of Years* (1995).

5   Consider several works by women which examine the subject of suicide. You might look at Kate Chopin's *The Awakening* (1899), Virginia Woolf's *Mrs Dalloway* (1929) or *The Waves* (1931), Sylvia Plath's *The Bell Jar* (1963), Marsha Norman's *'Night, Mother* (1983) or Carol Ann Duffy's 'The Laughter at Stafford Girls' High' (2001). You might also want to include in your consideration works by men in which women kill themselves – for instance Gustave Flaubert's *Madame Bovary* (1857), or Leo Tolstoy's *Anna Karenina* (1877) or Giacomo Puccini's opera *Madame Butterfly* (1904). Why do these characters commit suicide – or try to? In what ways are these works of social protest? In what ways are these characters responding to the pressures of a particular situation and a particular time and place? Do you think these characters might have made different choices if these texts were written today?

6   Consider one or more films written and/or directed by women. You might look at *Thelma and Louise* (1991) or Jane Campion's *The Piano* (1993). What elements of character, plot and theme do these films share with literature written by women? What do these films tell us about the historical period during which they were produced? In what ways does an understanding of the time and place depicted in the film help us to understand the character's difficulties?

7   Many women writers have chosen to explore the subject of friendship or love (or its absence) between women or sisters. Compare and contrast a few such texts. You might look at work by Anne Finch, Jane Austen, Christina Rossetti, Louisa May Alcott, Marilyn French, Angela Carter, Toni Morrison, Fleur Adcock, Adrienne Rich, Amy Tan, or Barbara Kingsolver. What sorts of affinities connect women with one another? What divides them? How do these authors use female friendship, love between women or sisterhood to develop their characters and themes? In what ways are relationships between women dependent on society, history, conventions and culture?

6 | Resources

Further reading

Rachel Brownstein *Becoming a Heroine* (Penguin, 1994)
A critical work which explores how women define themselves and their lives in novels, with particular attention to Jane Austen, Charlotte Brontë, George Eliot, Henry James and Virginia Woolf.

Cathy Davidson and Linda Wagner-Martin, eds. *The Oxford Companion to Women's Writing in the United States* (Oxford University Press, 1995)
A 'dictionary' of women's writing in America from the 17th–20th centuries. Entries on individual authors, and on social and cultural topics affecting female writers.

Margaret Drabble, ed. *The Oxford Companion to English Literature* (Revised edition, Oxford University Press, 2000)
A general reference guide to individual authors, movements and genres from the medieval period to the present.

Sandra M. Gilbert and Susan Gubar *The Madwoman in the Attic: The Woman Writer and the Nineteenth-Century Literary Imagination* (Yale, 1979)
An important study of American and British women novelists during this period.

Carolyn Heilbrun *Writing a Woman's Life* (The Women's Press, 1997)
A reflective and personal book which considers the ways women construct their own lives both as readers and as writers.

Mary Joannou *Contemporary Women's Writing: From 'The Golden Notebook' to 'The Color Purple'* (Manchester University Press, 2000)
An historical account of women's fiction in Britain and the United States in the 1960s and 1970s.

Vivien Jones, ed. *Women and Literature in Britain: 1700–1800* (Cambridge University Press, 2000)
An excellent introduction to the range and diversity of women's writing during this period.

Tillie Olsen *Silences* (Virago, 1980)
A collection of essays on female authors and on the challenges facing them as both women and writers.

Anita Pacheco, ed. *Early Women Writers* (Longman, 1997)
Examines the major work of important women writers of the 17th and early 18th centuries, including Margaret Cavendish, Anne Finch and Aphra Behn.

Lorna Sage, ed. *The Cambridge Guide to Women's Writing in English* (Cambridge University Press, 1999)
A lively and wide-ranging reference work covering the medieval period to the present and including entries on individual writers, specific texts, literary genres and movements.

Elaine Showalter *Sister's Choice: Tradition and Change in American Women's Writing* (Oxford University Press, 1995)
This critical work examines the relationship among history, culture and women's writing in the United States, with particular attention to the 19th and 20th centuries.

Alice Walker *In Search of Our Mothers' Gardens* (The Women's Press, 1984)
A collection of personal essays both on her own development as a writer and on black literature more generally.

Lois Parkinson Zamora *Contemporary American Women Writers* (Longman, 1998)
A study of women's writing throughout the 20th century.

Computer resources

Websites and CD-ROMs offer interesting new ways to access information about literature. A useful CD-ROM is *Contemporary Authors*, a source which offers brief biographical entries with commentary on thousands of modern writers.

The Internet has become increasingly useful for students of literature, and websites of all sorts and of every quality abound. A sample of some particularly fine ones for readers interested in particular topics or authors are indicated below. These sites can be especially useful in providing biographical and bibliographical information. Sometimes websites include E-texts (on-line reproductions of poems, short stories and even complete novels) or hyper texts (reproduced texts with scholarly emendations and commentary).

Suggested websites

Beginning Library Research on Women Writers
http://www-sul.stanford.edu/depts/ssrg/kkerns/womwrit.html
Presents both general and specific bibliographies of materials on women writers
accessible not only in libraries but on the Internet.

A Celebration of Women Writers
http://digital.library.upenn.edu/women/
Profiles an enormous number of women writers, covering 3000 BCE to the present,
and including biographies and bibliographies of female authors from countries
throughout the world.

The Isle of Lesbos
http://www.sappho.com
A rich resource for information about a large number of women writers from different
historical periods, offering bibliographies and examples of their work.

Literary Resources-Feminism and Women's Literature
http://newark.rutgers.edu/~jlynch/Lit/women.html
A site devoted to resources for women's literature, feminist criticism and gender studies.

Women Writers
http://www.womenwriters.net/
An informal but very useful site including book reviews, bibliographies, a chat line and
Internet links.

Women Writers of the Middle Ages
http://www.uh.edu/engines/medievalwomen/wmawma.htm
A good site to begin research on women in literature, art and music in the Middle Ages.

Glossary of critical terms

Allusion   an indirect reference, generally to a person, place or literary work, which enriches the reading context by calling up a set of associations.

Ballad   a dramatic poem, generally rooted in oral tradition, with conventional rhyme, metre, subject, and themes.

Bard   a medieval or Renaissance singer of generally narrative poetry.

Canon   a selection of texts generally regarded as essential to an understanding of literature. Since the selection has traditionally emerged from a particular group of readers (white, privileged, male) the question of how texts come to be admitted to, or excluded from, the canon is particularly contentious for women writers and women's writing.

Didactic   intending to teach, often in a rather heavy-handed way, conveying a simple moral message.

Dramatic monologue   a speech, either in the form of an individual poem or as part of a play, in which a single speaker, frequently unintentionally, reveals her or his character.

Epic   a mythological or historical narrative of heroic actions, often involving a journey and the struggle between good and evil.

Epigram   a brief verse describing a specific personality.

Epitaph   a short poem or few lines of prose, often put on a gravestone, used to commemorate a dead person.

Euphemism   the use of one word or words instead of another for the sake of politeness or in order to avoid being explicit.

Free verse   lines of poetry, without any regular metre or rhyme, which do not adhere to the rules of any fixed form.

Genre   (adjective: generic) a type or category of literary expression, such as poetry, fiction, biography, journal, letter, or diary.

Image a figure of speech in which the qualities of one thing or experience are attributed to another.

Industrial Revolution that period in western history, beginning about 1750, during which the balance of wealth and production shifted from a mainly rural, agricultural economy to a mainly urban, manufacturing economy.

Irony the contrast between what one might expect and what actually occurs. In literature, irony often depends not only on events but on the use of words to convey the opposite of their literal meaning.

Oral tradition literature, generally of an early historical period and before widespread literacy, whose texts were communicated by word of mouth.

Pseudonym a pen name, an assumed name used for writing, often in order to hide an author's 'real' identity.

Renaissance the period in western culture between approximately 1200 and 1600 during which the arts flourished in a way they had not since the fall of Rome in the 5th century.

Rhetorical question a question asked for dramatic purposes and to which no answer is expected.

Satire literary mockery, often for a particular political purpose.

Slant rhyme words which seem to echo each other, but not in any exact way, such as 'find' and 'pond', or 'fort' and 'heart', or 'try' and 'way'.

Vernacular ordinary speech, especially the actual language or way of speaking of a particular group or in a specific geographical area.

Index

ST EDWARD'S SENIOR SCHOOL LIBRARY

Acknowledgements

The author and publishers wish to thank the following for permission to use copyright material:

Bender Burrows & Rosenthal LLP on behalf of the author for Erica Jong, 'Alcestis on the Poetry Circuit' and 'Dear Colette' from *Here Comes, and Other Poems* by Erica Jong (1975) New American Library. Copyright © 1975, 1991, Erica Mann Jong; Carcanet Press Ltd and New Directions Publishing Corporation for Hilda Doolittle (H.D.), 'Fragment Thirty–Six' from *Collected Poems* by Hilda Doolittle (1912–1944). Copyright © 1982 by The Estate of Hilda Doolittle; Curtis Brown Group Ltd on behalf of the author for Margaret Atwood, 'Spelling' from *True Stories* by Margaret Atwood (1981) Oxford University Press, Toronto. Copyright © 2002 by Margaret Atwood; and for material from Margaret Atwood, *Negotiating with the Dead: A Writer on Writing*, Cambridge University Press (2002) pp.xvii–xviii, xxiii–xxiv. Copyright © 2002 by O. W. Toad; Faber and Faber Ltd for Sylvia Plath, 'Ode for Ted', 'Wuthering Heights' and 'Poppies in October' from *The Collected Poems* by Sylvia Plath, ed. Ted Hughes (1981); and HarperCollins Publishers Inc for Sylvia Plath, 'Ode for Ted' from *Letters Home by Sylvia Plath: Correspondence 1950–1963* by Aurelia Schober Plath. Copyright © 1975 by Aurelia Schober Plath; Sylvia Plath, 'Wuthering Heights' from *Crossing the Water* by Sylvia Plath. Copyright © 1962 by Ted Hughes; and Sylvia Plath, 'Poppies in October' from *Ariel* by Sylvia Plath. Copyright © 1963 by Ted Hughes; Emily Grosholz for 'Ithaka' from *The Abacus of Years* by Emily Grosholz, David R Godine (2002) p.81; Indiana University Press for Li Ch'ing–chao, 'A Sprig of Plum Blossoms' from *An Introduction to Chinese Literature*, translated by Liu Wu–chi (1966) p.116; W.W. Norton & Company Inc for Adrienne Rich, 'Poem XIII of Twenty–One Love Poems' from *The Fact of a Doorframe: Selected Poems 1950–2001* by Adrienne Rich. Copyright © 2002 by Adrienne Rich; and material from Adrienne Rich, *On Lies, Secrets, and Silence: Selected Prose, 1966–1978* (1979) pp.11 and 122. Copyright © 1979 by W.W Norton & Company Inc.; and Virago Press, a division of Time Warner Books, for Adrienne Rich, 'Compulsory Heterosexuality and Lesbian Existence' from *Blood, Bread and Poetry: Selected Prose 1979–1985* by Adrienne Rich (1986) p.38. Copyright © 1986 by Adrienne Rich; Hamish MacGibbon on behalf of the Estate of James MacGibbon and New Directions Publishing Corp for Stevie Smith, 'Papa Love Baby' from *A Good Time Was Had by All* by Stevie Smith (1937) and *Collected Poems of Stevie Smith* by Stevie Smith. Copyright © 1972 by Stevie Smith; Macmillan Publishers Ltd for Carol Ann Duffy, 'Anon', 'White Writing' and 'The Laughter of Stafford Girls' High' from *Feminine Gospels* by Carol Ann Duffy, Picador (2002); The Random House Group and International Creative Management, Inc for material from Toni Morrison, 'Spring' from *The Bluest Eye* by Toni Morrison, Chatto & Windus (1970). Copyright © 1970 Toni Morrison; Rosica Colin Ltd on behalf of the Estate of the author for Richard Aldington, 'To Atthis' from *The Poetry of Richard Aldington* by Norman T Gates, Pennsylvania State University Press (1974). Copyright © The Estate of Richard Aldington; The Society of Authors as the Literary Representative of the Estate of the author for material from Virginia Woolf, *A Room of One's Own*, Harcourt Brace (1929) pp. 11–13, 43–44, 48–50, 117; Sterling Lord Literistic, Inc on behalf of the author for material from Erica Jong, *Fanny*, Signet (1980) pp. 43–45. Copyright © 1979 by Erica Jong; Viking Penguin, a division of Penguin Group (USA) Inc, for Phyllis McGinley, 'The 5:32' from *A Short Walk from the Station* by Phyllis McGinley (1951). Copyright © 1951 by Phyllis McGinley, renewed © 1979 by Julie Elizabeth Hayden and Phyllis Hayden Blake.

Every effort has been made to reach copyright holders; the publishers would like to hear from anyone whose rights they have unknowingly infringed.